The Uncrowned Queen Reclaims Her Throne

When a Black Woman Breaks the Silence

By

Dr. Rev. Ahmondra McClendon

The Uncrowned Queen Reclaims Her Throne
When a Black Woman Breaks the Silence

Published by
Multi-faith Diversity Education
Carlsbad, CA

Cover Design by Lionheart Creations
Cover Portrait "Queen Ahana" by Maria Elena Cruz
Interior Design by Dawn Teagarden

ISBN:
Hardback: 978-0-9859364-7-1
Paperback: 978-0-9859364-6-4
Ebook: 978-0-9859364-8-8

Printed in the United States of America

multifaithdiversityeducation.com

*This book is dedicated to "The Uncrowned Queens"
trapped within the Legacy of Silence.*

Acknowledgments

A special thanks to my family and community who worked tirelessly and gave of themselves wholeheartedly so I could give birth to my dream.

Jewel Scott, my sister and #1 fan, for always supporting and loving me for who I am.

Stephanie Wilson, Aristia Lopes, and Capri Ashley Astwood, my great nieces for trusting me and having the courage to build new family legacies.

Vernon Oakes, My King and a light in my life who encourages and loves me unconditionally.

My dear friend Dr. Rev. Matti Dobbs Mavritte for holding my dream in her heart.

My Community

My Sistah friend, Albertina Lane who edited my work in the midst of physical challenges.

Amanda M., Vickie J., Marika E., Gloria T., Sharon J., and Kathleen D, the recovering Queens who cried with me, laughed with me, and had my back for 35 years.

My beloved sisterhood who held the spiritual space for The Uncrowned Queen.

Cynthia Bennett, Denise Benz, Alicia Soto-Goor, Lucretia Hayward Danner, Paula Joseph, Hazel Walker, and Dr. Rev. Ajene Wilcoxson for aways offering a listening ear and spiritual support.

Brother Ishmael Tetteh, for teaching, guiding and showing me the truth of who I am, what I am and where I am.

Sister Elizabeth, for Sistahood and helping me understand the African Heart.

Sister Grace, for showing me the resiliency of the African Woman.

For my Etherean Family who loved, protected and taught me the African Way.

The many blessed individuals who had faith in me and my vision.

The Ancestors who showed me the way when I was lost, provided the courage when I was afraid, and reassured me when self-doubt crept in.

Contents

Part III

Rewriting Our Narrative

Part IV

My True Narrative

Introduction

It was a Friday afternoon, and my week was almost over. I was feeling tired but also energized. My daycare children were all ready to go home, playing with each other while they waited for parents to pick them up. These little two-year-old's were the light in my dark world. Spending eight hours a day with these bundles of joy, happiness, and unconditional love was my saving grace.

This was the first time in weeks I was feeling a little joyful. Until my girlfriend called to say she was taking me out for drinks, I had been dreading spending another Friday night home alone with my jealous, sad, angry husband. His depression was unbearable and turned our beautiful three-bedroom home into a prison. My drinking and drug use had spiraled out of control as I struggled to live with a paranoid, emotionally unstable man.

Standing in the bathroom with the door open, putting on makeup, I heard him ask, "Where are you going?"

I hesitated before I replied, knowing my answer would probably start an argument. Me going or doing anything without him was unacceptable to him. "Betty and I are going out to celebrate her new job."

In an angry tone, he demanded, "Did you pay that bill and how can you go out anyway? You don't have any money."

Irritated I took a deep breath. "I will pay the bill tomorrow, and she is paying for everything, so I don't need any money." I was so tired of being interrogated, I blurted out, "Just kiss my ass!"

Instantly, I heard footsteps quickly moving toward the bathroom. Before I could react, he grabbed me by the arm, swung me around, and backhanded me. As my head jerked back from the slap, I saw the little ones looking up at us, laughing. They thought it was a game.

I knew fighting him was not an option. These precious children would not be witness to a physical altercation on my watch. They needed to believe we were playing. He backhanded me again, yelling at me to shut up. I screamed back at him, "Kiss my ass!" only louder this time. Holding me by the front of my blouse, he bent me backward over the tub. Thinking he might try to drown me, I needed to do something fast without panicking.

I knew he couldn't hold my total body weight with one hand because he was small in stature so I went limp. My strategy worked. When I felt his grip loosen, I jumped up and ran toward the bedroom. Realizing what I was going to do, he ran after me. I quickly retrieved the loaded 45 automatic he kept under his pillow.

Turning with gun in hand, I took the safety off, turned the barrel toward me, and put the gun between his two hands.

Blinded by rage, I dared him, "Shoot me right here, where I stand, because if you hit me again, I will KILL YOU."

In a flash, ten years of secrets exploded in my face. I was not a happily married woman. I was an abused, hurting woman filled with anger.

His act of aggression triggered the anger I had suppressed for decades, and it erupted with frightening velocity. And this anger wasn't just mine. For hundreds of years, my female ancestors had suffered abuse at the hands of men. All the anger we held collectively came forward to protect me that day.

That day, I was afraid for the first time. Not of him, but of me and what my anger caused me to do. No person in their right mind gives a loaded gun to someone who just beat them down.

I believe that God worked through my husband that day to put me in motion. I had been living in a prison of my own making, desperately trying to keep secrets about my suffering. Not only was I in an obviously unhappy marriage, grieving the fact that I would never have a biological child, and using drugs and alcohol to cope, my body was screaming at me to change my life through the painful diagnosis of Discoid Lupus Erythematosus.

How the hell did I get there—to a place where I felt so much pain and rage that the best option before me was my own death at my husband's hand? How had I, a Queen by birthright, been dethroned and silenced to the point that, in that moment, I was ready to die?

The truth is, that was my wake-up call to begin confronting the rage, the hurt, and the grief I secretly held within. Though I didn't have the words to describe it in that moment, some part of me knew that the Angry Black Woman who desperately dared her husband to kill her wasn't me. It was an embodiment of a false narrative—an identity—that had been scripted for me by a racist culture.

They had written the script, the cast of characters, and the plot twists in my storyline. Coupled with the inherited rage and code of silence from my ancestors led me to a moment where I had chosen to become the false narrative. Angry Black Woman is not my identity, but I am a Black woman who has justifiable anger at the injustices that my ancestors, my sistahs, and I have suffered—a Black woman who has been rewriting the narrative written for myself, and for us, for the last forty years since that dark day.

Truth is, I never intended to tell this story—my story—let alone put it in a book. But after thirty-plus years of witnessing sistahs suffering at the hands of this false narrative while working as a social worker, a life skills and purpose facilitator, a healer, and now as an interfaith minister, I guess Spirit decided I was ready to share my story so others could break their silence and rewrite their own. Of course, the Coronavirus plot twist seemed to be the perfect opportunity to apply more pressure—I mean, create the space—to do it.

The day the first coronavirus case was announced in New York City was the very same day I graduated and became Dr. Rev. Ahmondra McClendon. What an accomplishment! I was ready to launch my doctorate work—the Multifaith Diversity Educational program for social service providers I had developed over my three years in seminary. Determined to educate providers on the major Religions and the importance of incorporating (client's beliefs) Faith Traditions into service delivery, I had no idea that God had other plans.

I received a clear message that it was time to write "The Book." I knew exactly what that meant. For years, I had avoided writing "The Book," clinging to the excuse I didn't have time and I was too busy. But the truth was, fear stopped me from writing the story of my life. And just like that, my excuses evaporated when the world went inside and closed the doors.

Suddenly, all I had was time. So finally, I stood face-to-face with the daunting task of exposing my wounds to the world. Before I even began writing, it felt like the equivalent of standing naked on the freeway, allowing everyone to see the pain I worked so hard to keep hidden. That was scary. What will happen to me if I reveal all my stuff? Although my pain (from years of trauma) was healed, the thought of courting painful memories was enough to fuel my resistance. My motto has always been, "Let sleeping dogs lie."

Spirit reminded me that my story is a doorway through which another sistah's story can emerge. My story doesn't just belong to me. It is the story of women who look like me, feel like me, live like me, hurt like me, cry like me, love like me, and hope like me. If I tell my story, you may feel safe enough to reveal your stories. After much resistance, arguing, and maybe a few tantrums, I agreed to consciously break the Legacy of Silence and tell my truth so you may speak your truth.

I share a story that illuminates the tenacity and bravery our ancestors displayed in the face of unspeakable atrocities. A story that will cause you to cry, laugh, and self-reflect. A story that will escort you down dark unfamiliar roads you might be afraid to travel alone.

I offer this book as a tribute to my sistahs from the African Diaspora—those who cry silent tears while handling all that comes with being a Black woman existing in a racist society. Sistahs who veil their screams of pain within a Legacy of Silence. Those whose hearts break every time they see another mother's child killed. Women who feel the hot anger emanating from the secrets trapped deep within. The African American women who suffer the torment of feeling invisible or having their brilliance ignored. The ones who bleed within from the powerlessness they feel without. The sistahs who whisper in the darkness of night, "when is my time coming?" The Queen that feels her precious birthright was stolen from her and is desperately trying to find it. To the sistahs ready to replace that damn head rag with a crown.

I invite you to accompany me as I strip down to my core and take you through my personal journey of healing and transformation, but not before I show you how I was dethroned and what kept me from reclaiming my throne for years. As I have given voice to the various shades of my pain (ancestral, personal, and communal), I have been freed from the secrets and trauma holding me hostage. As you read my story of reclaiming all the parts of myself and my throne, my hope is you will gather the fragmented parts of your story and make them whole.

If you walk with me through our collective fear, hurt, and pain, we will reach a fork in the road, where a new pathway headed in a different direction awaits us—not just you and me as individuals, but all sistahs. Together, we can do what our ancestors could not do—break the chains of depression, weariness, sadness, madness, hopelessness, and powerlessness that exist in the Legacy of Silence.

It is our duty to face the anger we inherited and teach future generations to embrace the courage and resiliency they have inherited from the ancestors. It is also our responsibility to help them speak their truth. We cannot complete this important work while trapped in silence. By supporting each other, we can lovingly release everything blocking our path, reclaim our crowns, and live a fully actualized life. Come hold my hand and let's break the Legacy of Silence and speak our truth together. Because when one of us is free, we're all free.

What to Expect
Real Work and A Life Transformed

At the beginning of each chapter, a Queen is honored by a beloved descendant.

In Part I, The Legacy of Silence Unmasked, Silence is the Golden Rule; we will explore the inherited narratives that shape our personal stories. There, you will find stories from my ancestors that demonstrate the Legacy of Silence and how this pattern led to dysfunctional behavior and was passed down through the generations. This pattern of behavior is the broader view of what created the preconditions for my dethronement. I came by it, honestly.

In Part II, The False Narrative, The Queen is Dethroned, the psychology behind the Angry Black Woman myth is exposed. The significance of the strength, courage, and resilience our female ancestors displayed in battle and life is revealed. You'll also find stories from childhood and youth that shattered my innocence, tore me off my throne, silenced my voice, and strengthened my resolve.

In Part III, Rewriting Our Narrative, Claiming Our Throne, you will bear witness to my awakening and journey from being a scared, closed-down, in-the-closet drug addict to a powerful healing presence. You will see how God intervened in my world and created a perfect storm of circumstances that led to my transformation.

Causing me to move from pain to purpose, feel pride instead of confusion, and live from possibility instead of past memories.

In Part IV, My True Narrative, The Queen Reigns, I reveal the miracles I experienced on my journeys. And how those extraordinary events empowered me to step fully into my purpose as a Spiritual Healer. With my transition into Ministry, I received a powerful revelation. The reign of the Original Queen is upon us. It is time for Sistahs from the African Diaspora to reclaim our power and be a catalyst for healing in the world.

At the end of most chapters and sections, you will find questions to help you connect with your narrative and begin the journey of reclaiming your throne.

Our story is the key that unlocks the door to personal insights. Behind this door, painful life experiences are hidden. I call these events "Defining Moments" because, in one moment, we can create a story that defines us for life.

Our entire lives are governed by the narratives we create from life experiences. An experience can be so horrific that it throws us off-center, causing us to fabricate stories about ourselves. Once in place, these profoundly false revelations become the "Guiding Principles" that govern our life. The stories birthed from painful experiences become personal ideologies (beliefs) that guide our behaviors, shape our decisions, and keep us stuck in relationships and situations we know aren't what God intended for His Queens.

Unfortunately, we erroneously believe our stories are true, but they are not. They are woven so thoroughly into the fabric of our lives that we don't recognize they are false narratives of who we are. As a result, our authentic essence is hidden from us.

At the end of the book, I reveal an even deeper understanding of how my stories influenced my thinking and life in the Defining Moments and Guiding Principles section.

There, I have methodically identified the narratives I attached to my painful experiences and revealed how the accompanying beliefs I created put restrictions on my life. Then, as I reconcile my experiences (Defining Moments) with the views that they shaped (Guiding Principles), new stories (rooted in my truth) emerge, and my process of transformation is revealed.

My examples help you begin to make those deeper connections for yourself. Following my process, you can examine the experiences (Defining Moments) and personal beliefs (Guiding Principles) that have influenced your life. As you gain clarity, new stories shaped by truth will replace the myths. These new stories can be shared and become the legacy you are proud to pass down to future generations!

An invitation to The Original Queens Sacred Community is at the end of the book. I did not transform my life and move from victim to victory alone. I had six mighty Queens standing with me. For over thirty-five years, we nurtured, loved, supported, and encouraged each other to reclaim our thrones. I want to offer a sacred space of love to every sistah ready to reclaim her throne, create new stories and live as the Queen she is.

"Home affairs are not talked about on the public square."
African Proverb

Part I

The Legacy of Silence Unmasked

Silence is the Golden Rule

"Secrets" The Destroyer of Dreams

Fiery resistance (anger) wasn't the only trait passed down from our ancestors. They gave us the Legacy of Silence as well—a form of communication that ensured our survival during captivity. This bond of silence kept us safe while we cared for each other. It was dangerous to openly deliver messages, so we learned to use silence. Children were trained not to discuss what they heard or saw because their silence could be the difference between life and death for a family member. The Legacy of Silence became our way of being during captivity.

After physical captivity, the Legacy of Silence helped us navigate a racist world. When the night riders descended upon the Black community, our silence kept the nooses from robbing us of a brother or a son. When the welfare workers searched our houses for proof of a male resident, our silence ensured our monthly allotment of welfare payments continued. Our silence kept our precious babies safe from the grip of a foster care system.

For generations, Black women have nurtured our community in the Legacy of Silence. Our very existence is built upon this practice. We are the sentries that guard the doors to a world of unspoken secrets—secrets of pain and trauma we've experienced both personally and collectively.

Sistahs share a relationship with pain and trauma that is unique to us. Our strength lies in the ability to endure pain while moving toward our dreams. The drive to realize our dreams is encoded within our DNA. We stand on the shoulders of strong, courageous, and resilient women who walked through fire to reach their dreams.

Our ancestors gave us a legacy of reaching our dreams by overcoming. Overcoming the trauma of living with systemic racism. Overcoming the pain of living through personal dehumanizing experiences. Overcoming the burden of keeping pain-filled secrets buried deep within. Overcoming the desire to give up and let our dreams wither and die. We always look ahead because looking back is not where we are going.

As little girls we learn to keep our painful experiences secret and move forward, even in the face of no agreement. Unfortunately, the secrets we harbor erode the true essence of our dreams. And what we think is a dream is only an illusion of a dream that has morphed into a nightmare.

Often the price we pay for ignoring the pain-filled secrets we keep buried deep within is pre-mature death. We exit this world never realizing the destructive forces of cancer, heart attack, high blood pressure, stroke, fibroid tumors, severe obesity, diabetes, Lupus, and self-annihilation grew from the repressed anger, shame, sexual violation, unresolved grief, humiliation, personal loss, and violence hidden in our secrets.

Even before we die physically, we often die spiritually. Well-kept secrets break the connection to our divinity. We become divorced from feelings of compassion, morality, and integrity, leaving us with a distorted worldview that grants us permission to destroy life with impunity. Our life obsession becomes reaching that illusive dream, at any cost. Any cost to ourselves or others.

And maybe worst of all, we sentence our children and their children to the same fate.

We teach each new generation the unspoken rule: "You don't talk about certain things." It is imperative they understand that talking about painful secrets can embarrass us, slow us down, or distract us from the work we must do. It is our job to hold it together, regardless of what happens to us. The consequences we suffer are a small price to pay for the continued survival of the community.

Sistahs live in silence and endure behaviors that hurt us. Our endurance muscle has become the strongest muscle in our life. We endure and endure and then we endure some more. We wrap our endurance in silence because this is how we are taught to maintain sanity while living with trauma. We may appear to be doing well but that doesn't mean we aren't drowning in sorrow. We are exceptional at masking our pain. Unfortunately, we have developed unhealthy coping mechanisms such as obsessively working, eating, shopping, sexing, gambling, gossiping, exercising, smoking, complaining, arguing, keeping dysfunctional relationships, volunteering, co-dependent caregiving, and procrastination, all of which harm us.

Sistahs, what once kept us safe has trapped us behind a wall of painful secrets. It is time we left our prison of silence.

Were you taught to keep secrets?

How did keeping secrets impact your life?

Can you see the Legacy of Silence operating in your world today?

Did you ever ask why you had to keep secrets?

I hail from a powerful ancestral line of Queens. Women who made it despite facing impossible odds. Even though they cried silent tears and lived within the Legacy of Silence, they instilled dignity and pride in their offspring. The Legacy of Silence was just one trait they passed on. It is with honor and pride I share their stories of strength, resiliency, and triumph.

Mary Ann Rochester
April 17, 1902 - February 4, 1995

I called her Grandma, and everyone else called her Mrs. Rochester. She was tall in stature, always walked with her head held high, sporting a royal demeanor that screamed to anybody who saw her, "I am a Queen."

Her way was truly the African way. She believed in community and helped organize the Club (on the tiny island of Bermuda), a group of families that financially supported each other.

Grandma used anecdotal stories to teach and instruct. She was outspoken and, in a very straightforward way, wouldn't hesitate to tell you what was really going on with you. Need I say she was opiniated! In a loving way.

Thank you Grandma,

Your loving Granddaughter, Brenda

"We all deserve to have our stories told. And we all have much to gain by walking in other people's shoes."
Kerry Washington

Chapter 1

Grandma Mary's Story

Even though Grandma Mary was very secretive about her past and only revealed a little information about her life in St. Kitts, West Indies, it was enough for my sister and I to piece together her story.

Grandma had worked on a plantation as a young woman, where she'd been raped by the owner, a White man. She was a rape victim and my mother (Grace) was the result of that rape. Grandma wanted to love her daughter, but her love was tainted by pain.

When Grandma Mary's brother, Charles Brown, migrated to Bermuda and sent for her, the opportunity to leave her painful past was a blessing. She boarded that ship, suffering in silence, and arrived carrying an unwanted child in her womb—a child she would struggle to love. And a child who would struggle to be loved.

Grandma Mary disembarked on the small island of Bermuda and gave birth to her daughter and named her daughter Grace, for that is what God had bestowed upon her. A young woman who had no future in St. Kitts, West Indies was given the chance to break the chain of pain which was her life. Unfortunately, she had only added a new link to what would become a longer chain of pain.

Brother Charles loved his new baby niece and took great care of her and his sister. Gracie was the daughter he never had—his little princess. Mary and Gracie had a good life until Charles suffered an untimely death. One evening while attending bar in his establishment, he was stabbed in the stomach attempting to break up a fight between patrons. Although he was rushed to the hospital, the White doctors refused to treat him and sent him home, saying he was fine. Later that night, the beloved brother and uncle Charles Brown hemorrhaged to death.

The same White men who denied him treatment stole his valuable property from his wife. Mary and Gracie found themselves homeless in a strange country with no help. And once again, Grandma Mary was victimized by White men. Having no options, she did the only thing she could. She married a man who promised to take care of her and Gracie.

That first night of their marriage, Grandma's new husband told her to get rid of that "yella bitch." With tears in her eyes, Grandma Mary pleaded with her new husband, "You knew I had a daughter when we got married. Where is she going to go? She is just a little girl."

His response, "I don't give a damn where she goes. It just can't be here."

That night, Gracie became an outcast in her own home and a deeper level of pain for her mother. Her new stepfather hated the idea of housing the offspring of a White rapist and made Gracie suffer for it.

*Do you have knowledge about your
immediate female ancestors?*

How has knowing their stories influenced you?

*If you don't know their stories, are you
willing to uncover them?*

Grace Scott

February 14, 1925 - May 26, 2007

Gratitude to be in her presence

Realizing an Angel had been among us

Amazing in every way

Crystal moments is what you felt with her

Epitome of the Best Mom she knew how to be

Gracie, as she was affectionately called, never met a stranger. No matter where she went, she made friends. To her, community was everything. Every holiday she baked cookies and passed them out in the neighborhood. She believed in offering a helping hand whenever needed.

In her later years, she worked as a preschool teacher. The children and families brought her so much joy. She started making paper butterflies with the little ones and soon became known as the Butterfly Lady.

She distributed these butterflies wherever she went. If you went into the neighborhood stores and saw a paper butterfly, you knew Gracie had been there. In the local senior citizens center, her butterflies brightened the community room.

She was a firm believer in justice and advocated for the rights of the less fortunate. This trait she instilled in her daughters.

Gracie was loved by all. Her memorial service was attended by people of all ages and all races. She always gave sound advice, just at the right time. Gracie believed the purpose of life was to share and to receive love. She would often say, "A closed fist cannot give or receive love."

A Queen, she is truly missed every day.

Your Loving daughters Jewel and Brenda

"If you don't live your life, then who will?"
Rihanna

Chapter 2

Mother Grace's Story

Gracie Warner (my mother) grew up not knowing who her father was, never knowing she was the product of rape or why her mother's love was filled with pain. Her light skin and long wavy hair were in complete contrast to her mother's deep chocolate complexion and finely-chiseled African features. Although no one outwardly mentioned it, there were rumors Grace's father was a White man. She bore the pain of her mother's shame every day and struggled with their love-hate relationship.

When Grace and Grandma Mary lived with Uncle Charles, they were surrounded with love and acceptance. But his untimely death shattered her world. The new life with Grandma Mary and her new husband was filled with anger and violence and she learned to survive living with a man that showed her nothing but contempt and hatred. Her stepfather, Bulldog (his nickname), was abusive to everyone in the household, including her two brothers.

Grace went looking for love and acceptance, which resulted in teen pregnancy at seventeen. She was totally ignorant about life and had no idea what sex was at the time, and went along with the act because her boyfriend wanted it. When she announced her pregnancy, Bulldog made good on his threat and kicked her out of the house.

Her boyfriend was forced to abandoned her because his mother didn't want her son associated with a bastard girl from the wrong side of the tracks. It didn't matter that she worked with Grace at the Naval base laundry and knew her character. In this woman's eyes, Grace was unworthy.

Gracie found herself homeless with the responsibility of raising a baby. She left school and started working full-time to make a life for herself and my older sister, Almyra. Every day, she had to walk past her mother's house on the way home. If she was lucky, she could go in but had to leave before Bulldog came home.

One day it was raining extremely hard, and the stroller tripped over, throwing Almyra onto the muddy ground. When she tried to grab her, Grace slipped and fell also. Sitting there in the mud, holding her baby, she cried out to God for help. Although Gracie's life was tough, she did what Black women do when faced with insurmountable odds. She reached within, pulled on the courage, resilience, and determination from the ancestors, and persevered.

When Almyra was two years old, Grace's prayers were answered. She heard about the opportunity of a lifetime—one that could change the course of their lives forever. For a second time in her life, she received God's grace. The commander of the American Navy Base where she worked had been transferred to Oregon. He and his wife needed someone to bring their two young sons across country to them and the girl who was hired for the job couldn't get the necessary travel documents.

With only two weeks to get shots, a passport, and travel documents together, Grace managed to pull everything together and was hired as their nanny. She was faced with the most difficult decision in her life—to leave her daughter, Almyra, and create a better life in America for them, or stay in Bermuda and continue to struggle.

Grace (my mom) later told me, "I had to get off that Island because if I didn't, I would have died." As a teen mother, the community had branded her lowlife, no-good, worthless, not the marrying type. And the chances of living a happy life in Bermuda were minimal. Her greatest fear was following in her mother's footsteps and marrying a man that would abuse her and Almyra. Standing on the shoulders of her ancestors and pulling on their strength and courage, Grace left Bermuda.

She said, "My heart broke as I stood on the deck of the ship and watched my baby girl, waving good-bye to me." Crying silent tears as she sailed away to a new life in a foreign land, she hoped to create a life free of pain, where Almyra could grow up unburdened by the weight of her mother's shame.

Grace arrived in the United States completely and totally ignorant of the systemic racism infecting America. She had no knowledge about Jim Crow or segregation and proceeded to move through this world just as she did in Bermuda—freely. One day, when she got off the train and went into a White only restroom, a White woman came in and asked where she was from. When Grace started to speak in her heavy British accent saying she was from Bermuda, the woman welcomed her to this country and left the bathroom. She never told Grace she was breaking the law being in a White's only restroom.

Every time Grace was approached by a White person, and they heard her accent, she was left alone. Whites gave her a pass because they realized she was not a Black American but a foreigner. She traveled from New York to California by train with two little White boys and never saw the ugly face of racism.

In California, she lived with the commander where because of his status and race she was isolated from Black people. In her mind, there were no Black people in the United States because she didn't see any. One day she asked the commander where all the Black people were. He took her to the negro section of the base and said, "They live here, Grace."

The next day, she went back over to the negro section by herself. When she saw all the cars in the parking lot, she thought they were having a big party. She left, determined to come back the next day after the big party. When she returned the next day, the parking lot was still full of cars but she courageously walked up and knocked on a door anyway. An angel named Georgia opened the door. Grace looked at this smiling Black woman and her fear was dispelled.

She proceeded to introduced herself, "My name is Grace. I'm from Bermuda and looking for a friend." Georgia invited her in and a lifelong friendship began. When she asked her new friend where the party was because of all the cars out front, Georgia laughed and explained there was no party those cars belonged to the people who lived there. Grace was shocked because in Bermuda people drove scooters or motorcycles.

Georgia introduced Grace to many new things including James McClendon, a young handsome sailor. She fell in love and decided to stay in California instead of moving to Oregon with the commander's family. She and James married after Grace gave birth to a baby girl, Brenda (me).

Upon moving into her own apartment, she began a new life. Grace was happy and believed that life was finally working out for her. James was away at sea most of the time, leaving Grace alone, but she maintained. A White family in the neighborhood employed her to take care of their three children during the day, which gave her support financially and help with her new baby.

The other Black families in the neighborhood rejected this one White family living amongst them, but Grace didn't see anything wrong in working for them. After all it was her work with a White family that got her to this country. Even though she did not share the same history with her African American friends, she was clear White people were not her friends. She was clear about her role in their world. They were her employers.

When the city relocated her to a new federal housing project called Hunters Point, she took it as a blessing. She was within walking distance to the naval base where she had privileges to shop and receive medical care.

Grace was offered a job at my elementary school because of her active involvement, but her status as an alien prevented her from working. After missing that opportunity, she started the process to become a permanent resident. Working as a domestic to make ends meet, she always encouraged me to get an education. Her biggest fear was that I would end up like her, cleaning White people's toilets. She had bigger dreams for me.

Grace had no idea when she said the words "I do," she had started down the same path as her mother and the cycle of pain she so desperately wanted to end would continue. The beautiful daughters she worked so hard to protect would get trapped in generational and personal pain despite her choices.

What messages did you receive from your mother, or mother figure, about handling life's situations?

How did the females in your life deal with pain?

Did your behaviors reflect what you saw around you?

Almyra Joyce Smith

June 22, 1945 – Nov 9, 1989

Almyra, lovingly known as My, was a ray of sunshine. She was truly a lover of life. On the island of Bermuda, she was known for her friendly demeanor and her lively conversation.

Almyra loved her family, especially her two daughters, and worked hard to provide for them. Her greatest joy was when her youngest gave birth to a baby girl. Her granddaughter, Stephanie was her pride and joy.

As a loyal friend, she was there to offer a kind word or contribute to the well-being of others. Women would seek her out because they knew she would lovingly speak the truth even when it hurt.

Almyra believed in ancestry and worked hard to uncover her ancestral heritage.

She will forever be remembered and missed.

Love you Sis,

Bren

"Deal with yourself as an individual worthy of respect,
and make everyone else deal with you the same way."
Nikki Giovanni

Chapter 3

Sister Almyra's Story

Almyra was two years old when she watched her mother sail away on a big boat. She wondered why she had left her. In all her childhood, no one gave her an honest answer. Her grandmother Mary lied and said her mother left because she did not want Almyra. After years of repeatedly hearing this, she believed the lie, her mother didn't love or want her.

After Almyra's uncle molested her, they sent her away from the only home she ever knew. And so, she lived with two pain-filled secrets—her mother didn't want her and her uncle molested her.

Almyra grew up wanting one thing—her own home with a family to love and be loved by.

As little children, we all have dreams. Dreams are us tapping into our Divine selves, looking out into our world, and imagining what we can have. It's like walking into a giant candy store and someone saying pick out anything you want. It is yours—just ask. Dreams are exciting; they are what make life worth living. But something happens when we have a traumatic experience.

The pain fills our entire being and distorts our perception. We take that pain and try to hide it within a secret. But the prominent force in our life becomes the pain while our dreams become less vivid and move further away from us. Since we are Divine Beings, it is in our nature to want, joyous, happy, and love-filled lives, so we ignore the pain and pursue our dreams. Unfortunately, our dreams become distorted, causing us to engage in behaviors that don't serve us.

Almyra never realized that pain was her motivating force, not love. Although she was married, she believed another man would make her happy. Running from the pain skewed her perception. The man she wanted was not prince charming, but an abuser, and getting him would mean the destruction of another woman and her children. With disregard for them and herself, she ended up living in a nightmare disguised as a dream. Almyra's secrets had her seek love in a pain-filled relationship that hurt her and her daughters.

Have you ever made decisions from the pain you were feeling?

Did you have regrets later?

Almyra wanted a dream house that she could call her own. This dream house represented everything to her, and so she put all her effort into building it. But, in her quest, she ignored everything around her. She ignored her health and the doctor's advice. She ignored the physical and emotional abuse and put all her energy into building that dream.

That dream house became her prison and place of pain. She lived inside of it with a man who was an abuser. Almyra died four years after the house was completed. Her dream house took precedence over her life and became the house to die for. She died without ever understanding living within the Legacy of Silence blocked her escape from hell.

Have you watched someone you love put themselves on the back burner while they pursued other things?

Do you put other things in front of your well-being?

Have you kept your silence even when you wanted to say something because of your upbringing?

Sankofa is an African word from the Akan tribe in Ghana, which means, it is all right to return to the past and bring forward that which is useful. Using the way of Sankofa, past trauma and pain can be reconciled and healed.

Looking at our ancestors and the injustices they endured and suffered, we begin to understand how their trauma, pain, and anger have been important influences in our life. Reaching back to touch their pain allows us to reframe and relate differently to ours.

"Until lions have their historians, tales of the hunt shall always glorify the hunter."

West African Proverb

Part II

The False Narrative

The Queen is Dethroned

lack Women from the African Diaspora are the mothers of civilization. Science revealed that remains from a hominid skeleton—the oldest ancestor to present-day humans—are female and lived in Ethiopia 4.4 million years ago (Dalton, 2009). The next oldest hominid skeleton is also female, found in South Africa, and is 3.67 million years old (Bower, 2019). We have empirical proof. The African female is the Original Queen!

In many African countries, women were the King Makers. In other words, the women elders of the tribe choose the Kings. Additionally, the ancestral line followed the mother's lineage, making it a matrilineal society.

We lived in harmony with the universe's creative force and relied on it for strength. Every day, we embraced that connection, for it helped us do whatever needed to be done. Our life was devoted to uplifting, nurturing, and keeping humanity spiritually empowered.

We were protected and respected as mothers, daughters, wives, and sistahs. Our environment didn't exploit us; it nurtured us, allowing us to grow and develop into our ancestral role as Queen Mothers. And as Queen Mothers, we were revered.

Unadulterated American history reveals the truth: For generations, Black women from the African Diaspora nurtured our enslaved fathers, mothers, sistahs, brothers, daughters, sons, and the captors' families. The foundation for this nation was indeed formed from the blood, sweat, tears, and breast milk of the African Queens' descendants.

In the 21st century, her descendants continue to preserve our existence. The first immortal cells emerged from the body of a Black woman, Henrietta Lacks. With her DNA, modern medicine is improving and extending life on planet Earth. Civilization began with The Original Queens and is being sustained by her descendants.

With no recognition for our vital contributions, sistahs have been falsely labeled, treated inhumanely, and made to suffer in silence. A racist society dethrones us every step of the way. That dethronement is so complete we forget that we are the Original Queens.

A poem
Myth of the Angry Black Woman

Black woman—black woman
Don't you shed no tear

You better keep those words inside
and show that pretty smile

Black woman—black woman.
Who are you?
To have an opinion, must less express one

Black woman—black woman
You better protect your body

Black woman—black woman
I know you cry and hide your tears inside

Black woman—black woman
You are sad but you look mad

Black woman—black woman
Your hurt is all you have sometimes

Black Woman—black woman
The emblem for pain is your family coat of arms

Black woman—black woman
Deep anguish resides behind that mask your wear

Black Woman—black woman
I recognize your true essence

You are that little girl who sleeps with terror
You are that adolescent cloaked in hurt and pain
You are that young woman strangled
with the cord of rage and anger

You are the woman
Who is mortally wounded but doesn't bleed
The one who sucks it up, and moves forward in silence

Black Woman—black woman
When you spoke out, to protect your babies,
support your man
And reclaim the FREEDOM TO BE

They cringed in fear at the sound of your POWER
They labeled—your coat—dress- shoes—hat

The Angry Black Woman

Black woman—black woman
Do not suffer their label
Ignore the madness, acknowledge the myopia
Walk away
For they know not what they say

Black Woman—black woman
I see
Your pain, feel your hurt, taste your sadness

Black Woman—black woman
I see
You are kindness, Love incarnate, Courage in action,
Strength in motion

Black woman—black woman
You are not

The Angry Black Woman

You are
The Original Queen

Giving voice to her personal and ancestral **ANGER!**

The Angry Black Woman
A False Narrative

To obliterate our real identity (we are descendants of Queens), White men created a false narrative and put that label on us. That erroneous label sounded accurate because we were so angry (all the time) about so many things.

We were angry when we turned on the television and saw no one who looked like us. We were angry because Black women were ostracized for wearing their hair in cornrows, but when Bo Derek put her long blonde hair into corn rolls and ran down the beach, she was called a sex symbol. We were angry when we saw brothers leave sistahs and marry White girls, not because they loved them but because White society labeled them desirable—the forbidden fruit that became a status symbol. We were angry when White males (standing inside their White privilege) felt it was okay to comment on our luscious round butts. We were humiliated and enraged when they had the audacity to slap us on the ass and laugh as they did it—taking those liberties because they knew we had no power and would stay silent.

We were angry when they turned our brothers away from jobs because of their skin color. We were angry when Black men could not use their hard-earned GI bill to purchase a house in the country they fought for. We were angry when little Black boys were singled out in school as troublemakers, sent to special classes, and put on medication just for being little boys.

We were angry when five White boys raped a little Black boy in the school bathroom and suffered no consequences, even after the principal and school board members were alerted.

We were angry when we walked into a department store, and the security guard followed us around while our White girlfriends robbed them blind. We were angry when our sistah Angela Davis was locked away in jail, and we prayed that she didn't "accidentally" hang herself every night. We were angry when they blew up four little Black girls in Church while attending Sunday school.

We were angry because our community was powerless to protect itself from the many faces of systemic racism. We were angry when we saw drugs pour into our vibrant, thriving, loving communities. We were angry when we started burying friends at twelve years old, who had died from heroin overdoses. We were angry when we interviewed for a secretarial job out of high school, and the White owner took us around and showed us where all the garbage cans were so that we could make emptying the trash part of our duties.

We were angry when White women asked if they could touch our hair or if it was real. We were angry when White people said we were different from those others (negros) because we spoke so well. We were angry because White professors rejected our papers in college. After all, we wrote about the Black experience, and that didn't fit within their worldviews. We were angry because no one in class looked like us, including the instructors. We were angry because they never bothered to read literature written by non-White authors and therefore could not recognize the authors we quoted. We were angry because we had to go across campus to the Black Studies Department for our brilliance to be acknowledged.

We were angry because working in corporate America, we would see less experienced White women get promoted over us. The sistahs who became executive secretaries were light-skinned sistahs with long hair and white features. We weren't upset with them; they couldn't help their appearance. And they were also victims of racist policies. We were angry with the White men who wanted them sitting outside their office because they fit white beauty standards and met two quotas—female and minority. Along with a little extra bonus. Oh ya, baby got back!

Unfortunately, I bought the Angry Black Woman (ABW) fallacy and never questioned its interpretation or origin. But the day I heard a White male newscaster call a sister an ABW because she spoke passionately against injustices was the day I understood that label. He had deliberately ignored the issue she was addressing and put a negative title on her emotions. I realized he wanted to discredit her and stifle her voice. Clearly, the ABW label was a false narrative of who we were.

Dr. Wade Nobles, professor of Ethnic Studies at San Francisco State University, described power as the ability to define reality and have others accept that reality as their own. The ABW label is a powerplay to silence Black women in an attempt to define our reality and have us accept it as our own.

When fastened around our necks, the ABW collar becomes a gag order. It allows White America to avoid the real issues and silence Black women. Forced into a defensive position, we use precious energy explaining our intentions and defending our integrity.

Even though we're angry about many things (and justifiably so!), we are not America's definition of the Angry Black Woman. That label is not a representation of someone expressing anger toward injustices. It is a lie and a racist tool used to promote the false narrative that sistahs are loud, unreasonable, disagreeable, mean-spirited women with nothing relevant to say.

Our ancestors walked hand in hand with cruelty and barbarity every day, and it strengthened them. They were justified in being angry about the injustices inflicted upon them. They turned that anger into a powerful survival tool and passed it onto us. If it weren't for their strength, courage, and resiliency, the harsh conditions they endured would have killed them and denied us an existence.

In 2023, our anger feels no different than it did in the 50s, 60s, 70s, 80s, 90s, or twenty-first century. We're still fighting against the same atrocities perpetrated against African Americans that were present then and expressing anger toward a systemically racist society is emotionally healthy. It does not make us The Angry Black Woman. It makes us the Black Queen who is using her true power.

What is your gut reaction when the Angry Black Woman label is used to describe us?

Have you ever used that label to describe yourself?

Jacqueline Smith

November 30, 1964 - July 19, 2013

Jackie was one of those beloved people who would give you the shirt off her back. Everywhere Jackie went, she made friends and those friends stayed with her for a lifetime. Her infectious smile and laugh made everyone in her company feel joyful. She enjoyed traveling and meeting new people.

She didn't hesitate when she got an idea and would move towards that dream whatever it was. At the age of thirty-seven, she courageously moved to England and enrolled in school to pursue a career in public relations.

She loved her three nieces and worked diligently with her sister Freddie to make their lives comfortable. Although she didn't have children, she had over thirty godchildren. They loved her and she nurtured all of them.

Jackie inherited her work ethic from her mom, Almyra. She was never afraid to work many hours and often used her earning to support others. Never a dull moment in her life. She worked hard, played hard, and lived well.

Queen Jackie is missed.

"Anger is like fire. It burns it all clean."
Mayo Angelo

Chapter 4

The Battle Cry of a Baby Queen

At two years old, I was listening to my mom and dad talking, when something in his voice set off an alarm inside me. I had no idea what his words meant; they just didn't feel right. Something began bubbling up within, but my young mind couldn't comprehend what it was. However, it created an AW HELL NO! reaction in me.

I walked into the bathroom and grabbed the thankfully-empty metal potty resting under the wooden potty chair. Unnoticed by my parents, I marched back into the living room carrying the potty by one handle. Seeing that daddy was lying prone on the couch with his head on the armrest, I moved into silent action. Without saying a word, I raised my arm, and brought the metal potty down onto his head. BAM! (AW HELL NO!)

He jumped up, rubbing his head, staring at me. I remember my mother laughing and him saying, "Grace, that's not funny." Looking back at me, he chastised me. "Brenda, you shouldn't hit daddy."

His words meant nothing to me. I turned around, walked back to the bathroom, and put the potty back. That troubling feeling within was gone.

At two years old, I didn't understand the meaning of my actions or the motivation behind them. However, that wasn't the case at seven years old. I knew *precisely* what I was doing. I was defending my own.

As soon as I walked through the door, my young mind told me something wasn't right. The door to the birdcage and the window was open. Our beloved parakeet, Baby, was nowhere in sight. Daddy was standing at the sink, holding two gallons of ice cream we had just bought at the ice cream store.

Looking around the room, I asked, "daddy, where is Baby?" As he looked at me through bloodshot eyes, I smelled the familiar odor of alcohol on his breath. Then, glaring at me, he said, "You love that damn bird more than me." He turned back to the sink and started running hot water into the tubs of ice cream, pouring it down the sink drain. I knew this wasn't right; something was wrong with his behavior. It scared me, so I decided to leave. Grabbing a bunch of grapes sitting on the kitchen table, I hurried out the door.

We lived on the third floor and as I turned the landing onto the second floor, I ran into my mom coming up. She looked at this large bunch of grapes I had in my hand, and before she could say anything, I blurted, "daddy let Baby out the window and poured the ice cream down the sink." I could see the confusion in her eyes change to anger before she directed me to go back upstairs.

I didn't want to go back up there where daddy was acting strange, but what could I do? Stomach rumbling with anxiety, I followed her back into the house. I had a feeling something terrible was going to happen. I just didn't know what. Daddy was still standing at the kitchen sink with the water running when we entered.

Mom shouted at him, "McClendon, what are you doing? And where is the bird?" He turned around and just stared at her. "You need to leave and go sober up." With that, she turned and started to walk away.

I could see them both from my vantage point in the living room. Daddy standing at the sink in the kitchen, and mom walking into the hallway. Suddenly, he turned, grabbed a kitchen chair, raised it over his head, and started moving quickly toward her. *Oh no!* I froze. He was going to hit her with the chair. She couldn't see him, but something in me exploded, and I screamed, "MOMMIE!!"

As she turned around, she slipped and landed on her back just as he brought the chair down. Fortunately, the hallway was narrow, and the chair's legs caught on the walls, preventing it from reaching her. I watched in horror as she struggled to get up, and he struggled to dislodge the chair legs. Thinking he would kill her, I wasn't scared. I was angry, AW HELL NO! Something inside of me took over. Everything became crystal clear. I had to protect her. Quickly, I scanned the room for a weapon and spotted a large crystal glass ashtray on the coffee table.

As I picked up the ashtray, feeling the heaviness in my hands, my eyes focused on the back of daddy's head. He would not hurt her. I was going to bash his head in and stop him. This thing inside of me increased my strength and clarity of thought as I silently crept up behind him with the ashtray held high over my head. I was in motion when I locked eyes with my mom, who was looking up at me from the floor. When she saw the murder in my eyes, hers filled with fear. "Brenda! NO!" Her scream was like a slap across my face, causing me to freeze and snap back to myself.

Where had I gone? I realized I was holding this big ashtray high over my head, standing right behind my daddy. He quickly turned around and saw me standing there, poised to bash him in the head. I couldn't move or speak. As I stared at him, he also saw something unnatural in his little girl's eyes—something that terrified him. He dropped the chair and backed up toward the door. Eyes on me, he stammered, "I am leaving, I don't have to stay where I am not wanted."

My eyes continued to follow him while my mom scrambled up from the floor and grabbed a butcher knife from the kitchen. I was still standing there, ashtray over my head, watching this scene unfold. Mom waved the knife, threatening to stab him. Daddy tried to escape before he got cut up, disappearing out the door. Me? I was still in the grips of that powerful force, frozen in time and space.

Mommie rushed over to me, lowered my arms, removed the ashtray from my hands, and wrapped her arms around me. That's when my whole body started to react. I couldn't stop shaking and crying. She held me close and assured me that everything was okay. He was gone, and I was safe.

But it wasn't okay, and I didn't feel safe. Something powerful had taken control and moved through my entire body. I had no idea what it was or where it came from. I only knew it felt familiar, and that terrified me.

What role has anger played in your life?

How do you express your anger?

Do you suppress your anger to get alone with others?

How does anger impact your relationships?

How was anger handled in your household growing up? Was it okay for you to show anger?

I'm sure my inherited legacy of resistance was the motivating force behind my action.

My sistahs, we are the descendants of Queens who hailed from great empires. Queens who sat proudly in the seat of power and unapologetically spoke their truth. Queens who reigned with dignity, love, courage, and compassion. Queens who were loved and respected by their people. Queens who refused to stand down by always standing up.

Anyone who knows a sistah understands she will go to battle when it is necessary. Our bloodline carries the battle cry of "fiery resistance" AW HELL NO! Let a Black woman yell out, "AW HELL NO!" and it has the same effect as screaming "FIRE!" in a crowd. Folks start running because hearing those words means all HELL is about to break loose!!

Our ancestors Queen Nzinga Mbande and Queen Mother Yaa Asantewaa—two benevolent leaders, capable strategists, and fierce defenders of liberty—cried out, Aw Hell No! and went to battle after seeing the first colonizers kidnapping the sons & daughters of Africa.

Queen Nzinga Mbande, a brave fighter and brilliant ruler of Matamba, an African state, offered runaway slaves sanctuary, formed alliances with rival states, and waged a thirty-year war against the Portuguese. She evaded capture and at the time of her (peaceful) death in 1663, she'd developed her kingdom of Matamba into a mighty trading power (Bortolot, 2003).

Yaa Asantewaa, was appointed the Queen Mother of Ejisu and the Gate Keeper of the Golden Stool. No other female was ever chosen as Commander in Chief with judication over 5000 warriors. She led an attack against the British troops who held the fort in Kumansi, Ghana. Queen Asantewaa also believed in women's equality and spoke for women's emancipation. Her courage and loyalty are revered in Ghana to this day (Strautmane, 2020).

When our sister, Angela, arrived in Jamestown, Virginia (on the ship Treasurer), and stepped on solid ground, (I imagine) she looked around and said, "AW Hell NO!! This ain't right. I survived that treacherous journey, and I will survive this. Bring it on!" (The Angela Site, 2021)

When enslaver John Dumont made the mistake of refusing to honor his agreement to emancipate sistah Isabella Baumfree, she took her baby daughter and left.

Two years later (in 1828), after the New York Anti-Slavery Law passed, Dumont dared to sell her five-year-old son into slavery. Upon hearing that news, Isabella screamed, "AW Hell NO!" and proceeded to sue Dumont. She was the first Black woman to win a case against a White man in a U.S. court. Sistah got her son back and in 1843, she changed her name to Sojourner Truth (Fomer, 2018).

In 1856, Margaret Garner ran away, intending to use the Underground Railroad to escape slavery. However, finding herself surrounded by slave catchers, she screamed, "AW Hell No!" Rather than see her child destroyed in the horrific system of slavery, she courageously committed filicide, cutting her two-year-old daughter's throat (Nichols, 2007).

Our female ancestors weren't afraid to stand up and make a way when there was no way. Some fled at night from plantations, dug caves seven feet under the ground, and lived there with their children. Likewise, when we know something isn't right, we move to make it right, even if we must fight. We give the battle cry, "AW HELL NO!" and get busy.

It is no secret that our "crowns" were stolen. Still, even after they spiritually, physically, emotionally, and mentally raped us, silenced our voices, desecrated our honor, and stripped us of our birthrights, we didn't disappear. Although our very essence was traumatized, creating a disturbance in our souls and a distortion within our being, we stood firm in defiance.

Our DNA is coded to resist and we do, even in the face of imminent danger that arrives on our doorsteps cloaked in many disguises: character assassination, job loss, discrimination, imprisonment, domestic violence, rape, or straight-out murder. Our bloodline carries the strength of warrior Queens, and our battle cry, "AW HELL NO!" lives deep within. We know to express it even before we can speak the words.

Have you used the Battle Cry of Queens?

Have you been angry enough to fight against injustices you witnessed?

Were you taught about your connections to our female ancestors?

Fredricka Raynell Jabbar

February 27, 1965 – August 26, 2016

Fredricka was affectionately known as Freddie and warmed the hearts of everyone she knew. Her love for life was unmatched and she shone a bright light everywhere she went. Freddie took the time to connect with people and gave of herself regardless of their status. Her house was open to all, making anyone who entered feel loved, respected, and appreciated. She was a loyal friend and had relationships from childhood.

Fredericka worked hard and displayed the same love and affection in her place of employment. On her job, she was the face of her organization and promoted causes that uplifted the community.

Following in her mother's footsteps, she was a fierce advocate for the rights of Black people in Bermuda, always standing up for justice. Freddie embraced her African roots, even traveling to St. Kitts, West Indies, to research her great-grandmother's ancestry. Family was extremely important to her. Through her efforts, connections were reestablished with estranged family in the U.S.

Freddie loved her sister Jackie and together they share a special relationship. Her biggest pride and source of love were her three beautiful daughters. She was a fierce mother and defended them with her life. As a grandmother, she blossomed. Her delight in life was creating special projects and lavishing love on her grandbabies.

Fredricka left us way too soon, but her legacy will live on in all who knew and loved her.

"The most common way people give up their power is by thinking they don't have any."

Alice Walker

Chapter 5

It Didn't Have to Be This Way

When I was ten, my mother began sending me to spend summer vacations in Bermuda where I would stay between my grandmother's and sister's houses. Although Bermuda was a British colony, most people looked like me. Of course, there were White people on the tiny Island, but they differed from those at home. These White people didn't have the ugly attitude White folks had in America. Instead, I saw a world where Black people could live peacefully and prosper.

In San Francisco, most professionals I encountered were White. My teachers, doctor, storekeepers in the community, bus drivers, police officers, firefighters, and politicians were all White.

Bermuda was the total opposite. My uncles were skilled journeymen. One was a carpenter, the other a plumber. Mr. Bassett, the store owner, my grandmother's doctor, the minister of the church, the teachers, and the policeman were all Black.

There, Black people were known to be intelligent, productive, and worth something. Everyone lived in houses they owned. Whites controlled no public housing projects, and Blacks were free to move about without restrictions. I felt safe, respected, valued, and most of all free on this island.

As a little girl, I didn't know Bermuda's history and what Black folks had gone through to create the world I was privileged to enjoy when I visited. Eventually, I learned that their freedom was hard-won. They also dealt with the slave trade, being mistreated by White property owners, and the painful realities of segregation.

Bermuda was my example of what happens when systemic racism isn't the foundation of a country and policies are not implemented to thwart people's progress. The contrast between the two countries was astonishing to me. My summer trips were wonderful vacations away from systemic racism. Unfortunately, when I returned home, my status as a second-class citizen hit me in the face. Whenever I saw or heard terrible things happening to Black people, I thought it didn't have to be this way.

Have you ever experienced living or visiting a place where systemic racism was absent?

If you have, how did that feel?

Have you ever wondered what it would be like to live in a society without systemic racism?

Have you ever blamed Black people for our conditions?

Mary Eliza White

October 8, 1915 – July 10, 2003

My mother, fondly known as "Mae Liza," was the first of four children born on a farm in Alexandria, Alabama. Although she did not have a formal education, Mae Liza was one of the smartest women I know. She endowed me with something no school could offer, plain old "Mother Wit."

She had deep family roots and was totally committed to maintaining familial connections across the globe. She was especially close to her two brothers, James and Warren.

As a powerfully spiritual woman, her advice was always on time and needed. People gravitated to her because they wanted to hear what she had to say.

My mom and I shared a special relationship. She was my personal North Star. I was blessed to share a household with her most of my life. She is forever in my heart space.

I love you dearly, Queen Mae Liza.

Dr. Mary Rice

Chapter 6

Domestic Terrorism

I remember getting ready to go downtown with my mom. The day was beautiful. The sun was out, the flowers were in full bloom, and I was so happy. We went shopping to buy a new Sunday dress for Church. We always wore our best clothes for Church, as the Church was an extraordinary place. It was where we went to say "Thank You" to God. As I sat on the bus and looked out the window, I felt safe and loved.

When we got off the bus, my mom took my hand like she always did, and we started walking toward the store. As we passed a giant building, we saw hundreds and hundreds of people who didn't look happy at all. Some were crying, others were talking in loud and angry tones, and many were staring straight ahead. They all seemed so sad. When we stopped and watched, I noticed all of the people were Black adults. I didn't see any children at all.

My mom questioned a woman standing nearby. I couldn't hear what they said, but her grip tighten on my hand and she led us into the group that was walking slowly. After a short while, I realized we were walking around a big building. Because I was short, I could only see feet and legs, and even those looked sad. Their dragging feet made a squishing sound as we walked and walked and walked around that building for a long time. And now I was feeling sad, too. Something just wasn't right.

I tugged at my mom's hand, "Can we go now? I'm tired, and I want to get my dress."

"In a little while, we'll go." And we walked some more.

Then I got exhausted, and I had to go to the bathroom. "Can we go now? I wanna go!"

I will never forget the look on my mother's face as she looked down at me. Her eyes filled with tears, she gently pulled me out of the line and squatted to look me in the eyes. As she put both her hands on my shoulders, I could see the pain on her face as she searched for words to explain why we were walking—why we weren't going to get my dress today after all.

She wiped away her tears like she was trying to push her emotions out of the way so she could speak. "Last Sunday, some evil people set a bomb that blew up four little Black girls just like you while they were at Sunday school. We are walking today because we want those bad people to know that it is not okay that they killed those little girls."

As I watched the tears rolling down her face, I could only think about how much I loved my Sunday school class and Church. I thought about those little girls and how they probably loved their Church, too. And then it hit me. It could have been me in that Church. Fear gripped my throat, and I froze in time and space.

When we moved back into the line, I had changed entirely. I was not just a little girl walking with her mother. I was an angry little girl walking for justice. I stood up as straight as I could, threw back my head, and made a promise to myself: "I will walk, and I will walk, and I will not stop walking. It has to be clear no more little girls will ever be blown up again."

That day I walked and I never looked back. I never put my head down and I never got tired. I felt good, and then I felt happy again. I was walking to show the world those four little Black girls mattered. They were more important than getting a new dress; they were more important than me getting tired. I would never stop walking and forget the anger I felt toward those evil White men who murdered four innocent little girls in Sunday school.

That is also the day my hypervigilance began. I was always on the lookout for random acts of violence perpetrated by White people. We've lived in perpetual fear since Africans were kidnapped from their country. Descendants of enslaved people have memories of that perpetual fear trapped within their bodies. Although slavery was outlawed, the terrorist acts of slavery remained intact. As a result, African Americans not only live with inherited fear we also live with the fear from present-day acts of terrorism.

Even though White America refuses to acknowledge the many acts of terrorism against Black communities, they are real. Domestic terrorism is a way of life for Black people. At the editing of this chapter, ten African Americans shopping in a local grocery store in Buffalo, New York, were murdered by an eighteen-year-old White male with an assault weapon—in the year 2022!

When was the first time you experienced communal fear?

What caused it?

How did you deal with the realization that you were not safe?

Has fear impacted your physical or mental well-being?

Florrie Ellen Smith Oakes

December 4, 1921- March 17, 1999

My mother was a courageous woman. She enlisted in the armed forces to do her part in helping the country win the Second World War. For her exceptional service, she earned a Good Conduct Ribbon and received the WACC Service Ribbon for excellent service.

She could debate her point of view fiercely and won most arguments. As the mother of six children and one stepchild, she was always teaching. Even though my sistahs and brothers ranged in age from six to thirteen, Mom enrolled in school to better her situation. She set a goal and followed it.

Everyday she'd come home from her job on campus, help us children with our homework, fix dinner, and go to bed. Mom would wake up in the wee hours of the morning and together we would study our lessons. Through her example, I learned discipline.

Ellen maintained this rigorous schedule and successfully graduated Cum Laude from Bluefield State College. With a business degree, Mom took a position at the Mercer County Board of Education in West Virginia as an elementary school teacher.

Mom was known to many as a child of God and taught us about God's word and love.

She truly was her children's and grandchildren's heroine. And my greatest inspiration! I was blessed to have her as my mom.

She was truly a Queen.

Vernon Oakes

"It is better to protest than to accept injustice."
Rosa Parks

Chapter 7

Accidental Homicide

Laura, my best friend, and I had just stepped in front of my house when a school friend ran up to us and declared, "They shot Matthew Johnson." We looked at each other puzzled. Everything in me froze. That could not be true. We just saw him earlier that day. We were classmates in junior high school and every lunchtime, a group of us would leave school together. We'd go to a friend's house, eat lunch, dance, have fun, and return to school before anyone noticed we were gone. So, the notion that Matthew was dead couldn't be true because he had been with us that day.

We ran to our friend Marietta's house, the place where Matthew always hung out. We didn't know very much about Matthew. He didn't have siblings, and we had never met his mother or father. If anybody knew about this situation, it would be Marietta. We could hear screaming and crying from inside when we got to the house. Already knowing the horrible truth, we went inside anyway. Marietta stared at us through tears.

I was overcome with guilt as I flashed back to what had happened earlier that day. On our way back to school, Matthew had decided he wouldn't return with us. When I saw him break off from the group and go in the other direction, I called out to him, "Where are you going?" He said that he was going to hang out with Bacon, an older boy who was known for stealing cars.

I told Matthew he should return to school with us because Bacon was a criminal. "If you go with him, you're going to go to jail." Unfortunately, Matthew ignored my warnings and ran down the street. Unbeknownst to us, he found Bacon and they stole a car. Instead of jail, he ended up in a grave.

They were driving around the neighborhood when the police stopped them. Of course, they jumped out of the car and ran in opposite directions, but the police chased Matthew up and over the hill. As he ran down the hill, the police aimed his gun and shot. The bullet hit Matthew in the back, going through his heart. He died instantly, face down in the dirt.

That night, the community exploded. People were incensed and nothing could console them. The shouting from angry Black citizens drowned out the voices of politicians and ministers. Finally, a riot broke out and the National Guard moved in to gain control.

As the community erupted in violence, Matthew's friends suffered in silence. Our little group's world disintegrated because our friend was dead. We were in shock and returned to school the next day as broken children. We had no one to soothe us. Instead, as we struggled with our grief in silence, we watched our beloved community go up in flames of anger.

Matthew's best friend Terry was arrested and placed in juvenile detention after he took a knife to school and stabbed holes in all the basketballs. We were all so angry.

There were so many people at the funeral, I couldn't even get into the church—people we had never seen before. Many people and organizations exploited Matthew's death. Unfortunately for us, the funeral turned into a circus. They broadcasted his service on live T.V. Chartered buses and more than 200 cars went to the cemetery. They talked about Matthew's accidental homicide, but we knew the real story.

The pain was overwhelming. This time, the trauma from a racist act of violence took my vision entirely away, and all I could see was red. My anger burned within like a fire out of control, and it was getting harder and harder to contain. I wanted to riot like everybody else, break store windows, and throw stones at the National Guard. But I was paralyzed with guilt and shame. If I would have done more to stop him from going off, he would still be alive. I truly believed it was my fault Matthew was dead.

Three of us went down to where Matthew had been shot and spelled his name out in rocks as a way to memorialize him. That was our way of saying goodbye to our friend. We were left alone to mourn our friend, the loss of our community, and our innocence. The happy-go-lucky teenagers ceased to exist. At fourteen years old, I embodied the lesson: I am expendable. I lived in a country where a White police officer could shoot an unarmed Black boy in the back and have it ruled an accidental homicide.

Officer Johnson suffered no consequences. Mathew's murder was representative of this country's attitude toward Black people. The reality of systemic racism hit me hard: Black people in America weren't safe and conditions weren't getting better. They were worsening.

Have you experienced anger or grief at a young age
because of an act of violence by a white person?

Did you express the anger/grief or did you suffer in silence?

What decision did you make as a result of the incident,

and how did that decision influence your life?

Gladys Wallis Fermon Dennis

December 4, 1914 – August 6, 1988

Standing 4 feet 11 inches, Aunt Gladys stood tall as a giant and had a heart and loving spirit to match. Although she was the third child, she performed like the oldest. Taking care of her mom and other family members came natural to her. She was the matriarch of the Fermon family.

As a natural born leader, Aunt Gladys was brilliant at helping others reach their potential. Although she graduated from high school the great depression prevented her from continuing her education. However, after winning a contest, she was awarded entrance to the Madam CJ Walker school of cosmetology in Chicago.

After passing the civil service test, she went to work with the dept of Army in DC and encouraged her sister to seek employment as a secretary in the same department. When she moved to Oakland, CA her home on 56th St. was the place to be every Sunday where traditional meals and lively debates were plentiful.

Although Aunt Gladys didn't have children, she provided for her many nieces and nephews, always making sure they had birthday and holiday gifts. My mom loved her so much, I was given Aunt Gladys's name. Aunt Gladys is, was, and always will be a Queen in my heart. I feel blessed to be her name's sake.

Gladys Fermon

"If you are silent about your pain, they'll kill you and say you enjoyed it."

Zora Neale Hurston

Chapter 8

From the Frying Pan into the Fire

At ten years old, I understood why we finally divorced my dad. For years, we'd lived with emotional and physical abuse. He would lie and say he was leaving for sea, but he went to stay with his other family who lived less than a mile from our house. He even introduced his girlfriend and her son to relatives as his wife and child. When he was transferred to Hawaii, he moved them there instead of us. One Christmas, we couldn't afford to buy a tree because he stopped our monthly allotment check. And when we went on vacation to Bermuda, he tried to have my mom's residency status revoked, saying she had kidnapped me and abandoned him.

The stress we lived under began to impact our health. My mom's hair started to fall out and she developed large boils under her arms. Her suppressed anger would erupt in outbursts of verbal abuse toward me; but when my chronic stomach pain was diagnosed as a precursor of ulcers, things changed. That ancestral resistance gene kicked in and mom went to war. AW HELL NO! Her daughter was not going to be the casualty of a failed marriage.

Grace summoned her ancestral courage and ended her marriage. Even though she had lived in the United States for ten years, this was still a foreign country for her. Except for a few friends, she was alone with a young child to care for.

My mom's decision to maintain her British citizenship put her future in jeopardy after the divorce. She had never become an American Citizen. "I don't trust these White people in America, and what they might do to Black people. I always want to be able to return home to Bermuda." Thus, her residency was contingent upon being the wife of an American.

The decision to remarry was fueled by the fear of losing her residency status. Marrying Mr. Grier, a man from our old neighborhood, guaranteed her security. However, that decision changed our lives forever, and not for the better.

My mom was determined to ensure I didn't have a bad stepfather experience, so she planned outings to foster a bond between us. Mr. Grier presented as a suitable stepfather and even started to teach me to play cards. When Grace felt confident that he'd accepted me, they got married.

One night shortly after, I asked if he wanted to play cards and he said no. I asked the next two nights and he turned me down each time. Finally, the third time, I was walking away when I heard my mother say, "Now that you have me, you don't want to have anything to do with her. You just pretended to like her to get me." He didn't say a word in objection.

At eleven years old, I realized my situation had gone from bad to worse. I believed for a moment there was someone else (besides my mother) in my life who would help me, protect me, and love me. I was greatly mistaken. My stepfather was cold, distant and didn't care if I was around or not. We had unknowingly jumped from the frying pan into the fire.

Were you betrayed by an adult as a young person?

How did you feel and deal with that situation?

What decision did you make because of that treatment?

Did your decision carry over into your adult life? How?

I don't know why I was suddenly awake in the middle of the night, but I was. The wind was blowing hard enough to make my bedroom windows shake. Although the room was dark, I could see flashes of light in the corner of the closet. I figured the flickering lights were from the headlights of a passing car, but that didn't make sense because the windows faced away from the street.

Suddenly, my mom burst through the bedroom door, screaming, "GET UP! THE HOUSE IS ON FIRE!"

Looking past her, I could see fire blazing outside the kitchen window. I jumped out of bed and she helped me put on shoes. As I looked into the closet, I realized the flickering lights I saw earlier were actually flames. Grabbing a coat, we ran out the door.

The fire alarm I passed every day was on the corner by the bus stop. On my way to the fire alarm, I banged on the landlord's door, alerting him that our apartment was on fire. Then I ran and broke the little glass door and pulled the alarm.

On my way back from the fire alarm, I saw the landlord fully dressed, putting bags of money into his car's trunk. I wondered why he was up in middle of the night. Later, we discovered he had set the fire for insurance money. When I knocked on his door, he had already been waiting for someone to discover the fire and alert him.

I ran back to find our apartment, now completely engulfed in flames. Trembling with fear, I watched a fireball burst through my bedroom ceiling onto the bed. With it, my young mind exploded with the realization that only five minutes earlier I was in that bed. I could be burning alive right now. Something shifted inside of me. I had no feelings about my possessions burning up. What mattered was my life. I was blessed to be outside looking in, instead of inside looking out. Overcome with gratitude, I started to cry.

I heard my mother scream and saw my stepfather engulfed in smoke as he disappeared into the burning building. He reappeared carrying an arm full of his clothes. He had risked his life to save his clothes! Unbelievable!

There was a vacant apartment directly across the walkway and we moved in there. The Red Cross gave us vouchers to purchase new beds and some clothing and the neighbor upstairs who didn't lose their belongings in the fire loaned me a small T.V..

I went from having a room filled with everything I wanted to a room with a twin bed, a little table, and a TV.

I was in shock and lived in terror this apartment would also catch fire too, but this time I would be trapped inside. It didn't help that I had to see the burned apartment every day. Smelling the charred wood and seeing the black walls added to my trauma.

Did you suffer a major loss as a child?

What was the loss? How did your young self process the loss?

Was it a tragedy that turned into a blessing?

Did that loss have an impact on your adult life?

One night shortly after the fire, I was lying in bed looking at the little TV when Mr. Grier burst into my room, snatched the TV cord out of the wall, wrapped it around the TV, looked at me, and said, "You will never have anything in your room again." Then, he stomped out of the room with the TV under his arm.

I was stunned. What had just happened? What did I do? And then I realized he was being mean to me. I had exactly three possessions in this world and he was taking one away. I started to cry, not because I was sad, but because I felt powerless. I could not stop someone I tried to love from hurting me.

Once again, my mom was there to comfort me after a man in our life had hurt me. She spoke reassuringly to me, "Don't worry, we'll get some more stuff in your room. He's just mad because all his precious clothes got burned up." I looked at her questioningly but didn't voice my concerns. What about our stuff? It was burned up. What gives him the right to take his anger out on me? I was just a little girl.

Laying in the dark on that horrible night, I pulled up the same self-determination and self-preservation my ancestors embraced in the face of powerlessness. I vowed to never feel powerless again. I would not rely on others for my safety and well-being but create a life where I always had my own. I would be in control of my destiny.

Did someone take something from you, making you feel powerless?

As a child what did you do when you felt powerless?

Has feeling powerless influenced your life decisions?

What was the outcome of those decisions?

Phyllis Jean Thackston

December 28, 1955 – June 18, 2015

We aren't given the opportunity to choose how we arrive here or what our circumstances might be, however we can decide how we will handle those circumstances.

Although Phyllis was orphaned at a young age and became my mom in her teens, she pulled on the courage of the ancestors and fought her way through abuse and pain-filled situations.

With determination and tenacity, Phyllis raised me to be a loving presence in the world no matter what situations I might encounter. Because of her, I always passionately follow my dreams and look to God for the strength to keep going in hard times. She will always be remembered as a powerful Queen.

Denise Benz

"I'm convinced that we Black women possess a special indestructible strength that allows us to not only get down, but to get up, to get through, and to get over."

Janet Jackson

Chapter 9

Innocence Stolen

Mr. Grier didn't work far from my school and would drop me off on his way to work each day. I would meet my best friend, Laura, on the corner and we would enter school together. One particular morning, Mr. Grier and I started our journey like every other morning.

We usually made the trip in silence, but today was different. He started asking me questions. "Is tomorrow a school holiday?" I confirmed that it was. "Does your mother have to work?" I affirmed that too. Then he asked me the weirdest question—a question that made me cringe and move closer to the passenger door. "Do you know what sex is?" The hair on my neck stood up. Something inside of me shouted, "DANGER! DANGER!"

I quietly said, "No," and then a memory surfaced. He was always accusatory and trying to discredit me in my mom's eyes every chance he got, labeling me as "fast." Back in the day, if a girl was "fast," she was a bad girl that let boys do things to her. In one of his reputation bashing sessions, he said I use to get with the little boys. I wondered if that is what he was talking about—sex?

He stopped asking questions but continued to talk. "Tomorrow, when your mother goes to work, I want you to take a nice shower, come into the bedroom, and I'll teach you what sex is all about."

That was the last thing I wanted to do. My mother had trained me to stay away from strangers because they might hurt me, but he wasn't a stranger. Smiling at me, he instructed, "Don't tell your mother about this. It'll be our little secret." Those words confirmed what I was thinking—I was in trouble. If this was a secret, then what he wanted to do was wrong and would hurt me.

He dropped me off at school like nothing had happened, confident that I would not say anything. The moment I saw my friends waiting for me on the corner, I broke down sobbing. My best friend, Laura, looked at me shocked, "What's wrong with you?" I could barely talk but eventually managed to tell her what Mr. Grier had said between sobs. Her face changed and her voice was stern. "You are going home right now to tell your mother."

I went into a panic. "No, no, I can't tell my mother."

She raised her voice. "YES, YOU CAN! And we are taking you home RIGHT NOW!"

My other girlfriend, (who was older than us) had her father's car that day, so they put me in the car and we drove in silence to my house.

I was terrified as we approached my house. I didn't know why I didn't want to tell my mother because I hadn't done anything wrong. Maybe it was because of her rule, "You don't tell secrets." But if I didn't tell her, the next day would be a bad day for me.

Laura walked me through the gate and pushed me toward the front door. "I will wait right here for you. Now go!"

I unlocked the door, stepped inside, and found my mom in the hallway.

Staring at me, she asked, "What are you doing here?"

I started crying hysterically and she grabbed me by the shoulders and slapped me across the face to bring me back from my hysteria. It did the trick. I struggled, but I told her everything. And as I talked, I watched her eyes glaze over. She calmy said, "Go back to school." That's all she said, and I left.

I found out much later that after I left, she called Mr. Grier's job and had him sent home for an emergency. When he got there, she threatened to kill him if he ever said anything again to me. He suddenly understood that if he wanted to live, teaching me about sex was not going to happen in his lifetime.

Even though my best friend saved me from what could have been years of physical sexual molestation, Mr. Grier had emotionally violated me. He'd taken something very precious from me, my innocence, and my safety. I was left feeling vulnerable and alone and I didn't dare tell my father. I didn't want to deal with a dead stepfather, a grieving mother, an incarcerated dad, and a hysterically vindictive stepmother. It wasn't worth it. I swallowed my pain and stayed silent.

After that disastrous day, I hid in my room if my mom wasn't home. One day, when I was alone in the house with him and I saw the doorknob to my room turning, and I quietly slid into the walk-in closet. He opened the door and looked around. When he didn't see me, he closed the door. I threw some clothes into a bag and, when he wasn't looking, I left the apartment and ran away to my friend's big sister's house. She let me stay there.

I wanted my mother to leave Mr. Grier. We could do well without him like we did before she married him and I couldn't fathom how she could stay with him after what he did to me. However, my friend's sister explained I was putting my mom in a terrible position. I was asking her to choose between her husband and her daughter, and she could not do that. Her very existence depended on her marriage. Without it, she could be forced to leave this country. Realizing our situation was hopeless, I acquiesced and returned home. The incident became the elephant in the room that was never discussed.

Each passing day my determination to get out of that house increased. I felt unsafe and angry because once again I was powerless to do anything about my situation. When my inherited anger merged with my personal anger, I changed. The sweet innocent girl quietly went away (with her secret), and a goal driven, angry, no-nonsense young woman with one objective—become powerful—took her place.

Have you been violated? Who was the perpetrator?

How did that experience impact your life as a female?

Did you tell anyone about that experience?

If you did, what happened?

Did you heal from that experience or hide the pain within a secret you carry with you?

Juanita E. Young-Miles

September 7, 1949 – September 1, 2019

Juanita was our resident actress. She loved performing and had the opportunity to be in several productions. In the seventies, she graced the billboards as the pretty Black girl in the Kool cigarette ads. She was proud about her role in the original horror movie, The Body Snatchers. Juanita enjoyed working with Michael Douglas on the police series, The Streets of San Francisco.

In later years, Juanita served on the Commission of The Status of Women of San Francisco. She was an advocate for women's rights. Juanita took her fight all the way up to Washington DC, where she spoke to the Bush administration on behalf of women and children.

She found joy in raising her two sons and was elated when she became a grandmother.

Juanita was also a proud member of narcotics anonymous. She felt blessed to have found a way to recover from her powerful crack cocaine addiction. Working in programs to help and support other addicts, she became instrumental in the lives of those struggling with active addiction.

Juanita was a true and loyal friend with a laugh that could pierce even the hardest of hearts. This Queen is surely missed.

Your friend and sponsor,

Brenda M.

Chapter 10

The Death of a Community

Unfortunately, Black children often face death prematurely because of the situations occurring in their communities. In addition to losing my schoolmate Matthew in junior high, I also lost a thirteen-year-old neighbor to a heroin overdose. We walked into the funeral home to attend his wake and when I looked into the casket, I was confused. The person lying there looked to be in his twenties. He couldn't be my friend. So I went back and looked at the name on the marque to make sure this was Michael Griffin. It was.

My friend Lillie and I had spent many days hanging out at her home. Then, one day Lillie went missing. Her bloated body was discovered several days after laying out in the sun from a heroin overdose. She left two little children motherless.

What was once a vibrant, loving community transformed into the land of the living dead. I stood helplessly by and watched with sadness as my community declined.

The White power structure in America uses herculean efforts to maintain the status quo. The wheel of systemic racism rolls over anything that appears to threaten its absolute power. For it to continue in force, it must keep others down.

When the African American community became a real threat to the status quo, White America developed a new war strategy. Destroy the African American community from within. And almost overnight, drugs flowed freely into the community. The first drugs I saw unloaded into the community on a mass scale were pharmaceutical drugs in pill form, specifically tranquilizers. These drugs put us into a chemical-induced coma.

Black youth got access to jars of pills to sell in high school, and we started taking them. We also started overdosing from them. One day, I reported on two students who tried to hide an unconscious girl in the bathroom. They didn't want her to get in trouble; I didn't want her to die. She lived, but I was labeled a snitch!

The thing with tranquilizers is you could forget how many you took and continue to take them. I almost became a drug overdose victim when I took too many pills and slept for three days. Then, by the grace of God, I woke up. Another friend wasn't as lucky. She died from an overdose of pills. The day she was buried, her brother was on the corner selling the same drugs that killed her. When we confronted him, he said it was her fault she died. No one told her to take that many pills!

The next drug unloaded into the community was heroin. One day there was no heroin in the community, and the next day, my friends started dying of heroin overdoses.

The ugly face of systemic racism killed the communities' spirit, destroying the motivation of many, who tried to change things. After Matthew's murder, a small group of us decided to join the movement and do something about the injustices happening in our community. We became activists and formed a youth chapter of the NAACP called, The Nat Turner Activist. Organizing other youth in Hunters Point, we followed the path of nonviolent resistance promoted by Rev. Dr. Martin Luther King Junior. We marched and participated in sit-ins, but nothing seemed to stem the tide of violence against our community.

We had all grown up in the church, however some started to rejected Christianity. The image of a White Jesus seemed contradictory. Why would we worship someone who looked like our oppressors? The Nation of Islam became the new religious home for some. We gravitated toward the Black Panther Party and were encouraged by the messages of Malcolm X.

It appeared that Black people were finally going to become self-sufficient and use their talents to uplift the Black community. We put down the "Negro" label and picked up the mantel of Black Pride. The more our nonviloent protest were met with violence, the more we worked to create change.

At every turn, systemic racism undermined our efforts and we hated it. Disillusionment started to set in when the Black Panther party came under attack by the FBI. After the assassination of el-Hajj Malik el-Shabazz (Malcolm X) and Martin Luther King Jr., our hopes for creating a world of prosperity for the Black community started to fade.

Liberation felt empty because we were powerless to stop the injustices perpetrated against our communities. When empowerment programs were eliminated and over-policing in the community increased, anger and bitterness filled the hearts of our group.

During these turbulent times, it was no coincidence movies like Super Fly glorifying drug dealers were released. Selling drugs became the new "Black Capitalism." It was the easiest and quickest way to get out from under the "Mans' foot, beating him at his own game." Cocaine dealers and pimps were glamorized and held up as role models. While our brothers and sistahs in the struggle were discredited, killed, beaten, jailed, or chased into self-imposed exile.

Our group struggled to stay faithful in our activism, but after years of marching, protesting, and fighting, the vision for a new future evaporated. We rightly complained that the system kicked and beat us back four steps for every two steps we took forward. We saw no end to the policies held in place by systemic racism. Everything in America was designed to hold us in bondage.

Our group finally disbanded with each of us going in different directions. It was unfortunate but several ended up statistics— jailed for drugs sales, overdosed from drugs, or murdered. The trauma of witnessing the death of my community, and demise of my friends turned into more pain I learned to live with silently.

How do you process the pain of constantly seeing brutality perpetuated against the community?

Does it make you feel powerless?

Have you witnessed friends or relatives becoming a statistic?

What decisions did you make as a result?

Miriam Heyward

October 18, 1932 – December 23, 2015

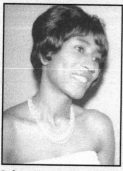

Miriam Heyward was a very sweet and genuinely loving daughter, sister, friend, grandma, and most importantly for me, mom.

She was born in Charleston, South Carolina, and enjoyed her southern roots and traditions. Whatever Miriam did, she did it with style. In high school, she led the band as a Majorette. When newly married, she traveled to Los Angeles and started our family.

It became apparent she was born to live in California, especially in LA. Her beauty often had her mistaken for someone famous. Unbeknownst to those who were drawn to her like a moth to a flame, it was her Divine Light and Love that shone so brightly, authentically, and sublimely.

She was an accomplished bowler, a talented roller skater, a true fashionista and a trained Cosmetologist. Creating beauty for herself, our family, and others was her passion. My mom enjoyed the gathering of friends, good music, cooking delicious food, fine dining, attending theatrical performances, and celebrating family. And most of all, she put family first.

Miriam stood for honesty, forthrightness, courage, compassion, empathy, commitment, loyalty, having a forgiving heart, and doing one's best. How blessed am I to carry the legacy of one who taught me so much, loved me unconditionally, believed in me and encouraged me by just being. Miriam will always be cherished. She is a Queen.

Lucretia Heyward Danner

"I am the sole author of the dictionary that defines me."
Zadie Smith

Chapter 11

I Know Who I Am!

The day was "Youth in Government Day" in San Francisco and I represented my high school as The City Treasurer. I was about to enter that unknown world of Whiteness, and every cell in my body was on edge. My mom dressed me superbly. Unfortunately, while I looked great on the outside, on the inside I was in shambles. As I sat on the bus that early cloudy, drizzly morning, I looked at the people around me. I was terrified and alone, but no one seemed to notice.

Growing up in public housing, I lived with the same values and morals as my ancestors. The African proverb it takes a village to raise a child was the blueprint for upbringing. I was everyone's child and was cared for by all the adults in the community. When my mother went to her domestic job, the woman upstairs who we called grandma looked out for me. When my friends across the hall were home alone, my mom looked out for them. If tragedy hit one family, everyone came to their aid. The term "latchkey kid" didn't exist in my world.

African Americans live in two worlds. We are understood, celebrated, loved, and nurtured in the Black world. This is our safe place. However, in the White world, we are invisible and only acknowledged when we can provide a service. Therefore, an African American child who learns about White supremacy in the comfort of their community is blessed. Because, as experiential learning, White supremacy delivers painful life lessons.

In San Francisco, there were two African American communities, Hunters Point and Fillmore. We had everything within our communities and no reason to enter White communities. I was familiar with White communities because my mother was a domestic, but I was still taught not to venture into those areas. It wasn't safe. So today, I was going into hostile territory.

I had never been to City Hall, and now I would be the acting City Treasurer for one day. Everyone told me how lucky I was and this was a great opportunity; however, their words were hollow and didn't comfort me. As I boarded the second bus that would deliver me to City Hall, I had a panic attack. My knees started to shake, and I began to feel sick.

I jumped off the bus at the next stop and ran into the Woolworth store where I sat at the lunch counter and ordered a tea to steady my nerves. I stared at the countertop, wishing I could disappear.

Suddenly, I heard a friendly voice and looked up into the face of a White waitress. She had big hair and bright red lips sporting the biggest smile. Her smile warmed my heart and took away my feelings of aloneness. "Cheer up, honey. Things can't be that bad." I offered her a weak smile. That anonymous sweet lady gave me the courage to get off that stool and continue my journey to City Hall.

Clutching my purse, I approached City Hall, determined to be okay. There was a steady line of cars dropping off other kids and my heart sank as I realized no one looked like me. I walked into the reception room, desperately looking for a familiar face. Disappointed again. Out of two hundred high school kids, ten were African American. We acknowledged each other with that "I am happy to see another Black face" nod. We looked so uncomfortable because we felt out of place. I knew we all had the same wish swirling around inside. We were hoping that Judge Kennedy was our city government official. He was the only African American in city government, and being with him would be a blessing. We would feel safe with him.

No such luck for me.

I was escorted down the hall to meet Mr. Tax Assessor, a White man. When his secretary called to him that his student replacement had arrived, he came out of his office with a big smile that vanished when he saw me. He exchanged glances with his aide, and I read the disappointment in his eyes. Nevertheless, he was cordial to me for all of five minutes, introducing me to the only minority person on his staff, a pretty Latino woman. Then, he quickly dismissed me to his aide and disappeared back into his office. I never saw Mr. Tax Assessor again.

Around mid-morning, I went across the street to have coffee and donuts with four local White male politicians. When we walked into the coffee shop, everything stopped. The people stopped talking. The servers stopped serving. Even the coffee being poured stopped in midair. All eyes were fixed on this little Black girl surrounded by four White men. I squared my shoulders, locked my knees, pushed my head up, and glided across the floor with the biggest smile on my face. When we reached our table, the coffee started pouring, everyone started talking, and the servers returned to serving.

The conversation was light and superficial, and then it turned toward me. "Well, Brenda, what do you want to do when you finish high school?"

I was happy to be included. Now was my chance to engage, show my intelligence, and share my dream. "I like psychology and I like to work with children. I want to be a child psychologist," I declared proudly. You would've thought I had slapped them because their faces turned beet red.

After recovering from my announcement, they exchanged quick looks, and one man cleared his throat before speaking. "My son is a child psychologist." My ears perked up as I thought some encouragement was forthcoming. Then another chimed in, "Brenda, you seem to be a very bright girl. You would probably make a good secretary."

Did he just dismiss what I said and offer me something less? A good what? How dare you! Your son can be a child psychologist, but I can't. So HOW DARE YOU TRY TO DISSUADE ME FROM MY DREAM!

I was FURIOUS, but the words coming out of my mouth were said calmly and with conviction, "Oh yes, I would make a good secretary. But I am going to be a child psychologist." There, I said it! I rejected your racist remark! You implied I couldn't; I said I would. Good for me!

The tone at the table changed immediately. I could intuitively hear the conversation running through their minds. Who is this uppity nigger girl to think she can be more than a secretary? Then they started to play the invisible game with me. You know—talking like I wasn't there. But I didn't care. I had made my stand. So I sat silently, sipped my tea, and thought how relieved I would be when the day was over.

As the day rolled on, I longed for something to validate my existence. On several occasions, I wanted to scream, "I am here. I know who I am; I am somebody who matters." I was grateful when lunch finally rolled around. Only one more hour and I would be free from this alien land. I sat at a table with two other White students who looked more bored than me.

The student mayor for the day would give the keynote address, but I wasn't interested in who was speaking or what would be said. He was going to be another White student from a wealthy family, expounding the virtues of City Government. Blah! Blah! Blah! I was emotionally exhausted like I had been in a fight all day defending my existence. All I wanted to do was leave City Hall and put this whole day behind me.

The real mayor introduced the student mayor and as everyone applauded, I swung my chair around to look toward the stage. I was awestruck. My mouth fell open, my eyes widened, and my whole body swelled with pride. I was looking at the student mayor for a day and he looked just like me! His skin was mocha chocolate, and with his full lips and his parted afro, he represented us—he represented me. He was the most articulate, well-versed young man in the place and I loved him for that. With him, we would be counted on this day. So I sat in my seat smiling and thought, "Look out, world, because here we come!"

That day my determination to succeed was reinforced. No matter what White America said or did to dissuade me, I would never stop advancing. In that wonderful moment, I could feel the courage of my ancestors surging through my blood.

When I reached voting age, I helped move Mr. Tax Assessor out of city government and into retirement. Although I did not become a child psychologist or a secretary, I did become a Professional Social Worker. The wheels of change do move slowly. Even though it took fifty years, in 2018, I was blessed to witness London Breed, an African American female, become the Mayor of San Francisco.

Has your self-worth been put in question by a White person?

When did it happen?

Have you ever questioned your self-worth?

Laura Catherine Rivers
October 31, 1952 – August 11, 1973

Laura was nicknamed "Granny" by her friends because of the round frame glasses she wore. No one could have a more true or loyal friend. She always looked out for her friends and whatever opportunity she saw for them, she passed it on.

Her dream to become a licensed barber was realized in 1972 when she became one of the youngest females in San Francisco to work in that male-dominated field. Having a deep understanding about the impact of systemic racism on the community, she was an advocate for justice at a very young age. Laura was determined to change things in a country where little black girls weren't always safe.

Although she was small in stature, her heart was big. She is remembered for having a gentle spirit and kind heart. Although she left us at a very young age, her memory remains in the hearts of all who knew and loved her.

I miss you, Queen Laura.

Your BFF,

Brenda

"We must cease being participants in our own oppression."
Stacey Abrams

Chapter 12

A Self-fulfilling Prophecy

I stood in the crowded department store fighting back tears. It was incomprehensible. Here I was trying to pick out a dress to bury my best friend in. The dress needed a very high collar to cover the burns on her neck made from the telephone cord used to strangle her. It also needed long sleeves to hide the needle marks in her arms made from injecting heroin.

When Laura forced me to reveal Mr. Grier's plan to molest me, she expressed an anger and urgency I didn't understand. Unbeknownst to me at the time, she had been sexually molested by her biological father. When she saw the same thing about to happen to me, she stepped in and protected me. Unfortunately, no one had protected her. That secret had haunted her very existence, destroyed her self-worth, and put her on a path to self-destruction. Even though she desperately tried to live a "normal life," keeping this secret overshadowed any accomplishments she made. Graduating from high school and becoming a licensed barber didn't soothe her troubled soul and no amount of alcohol or drugs removed the pain she held within.

In Laura's desperation to feel worthy, she had surrendered to a lifestyle she knew would eventually kill her. It's hard to understand how selling drugs and prostitution could promote feelings of self-worth; but when you feel unworthy, attention and praise from anyplace is welcomed. She once confided in me that nothing mattered because she would never live to see twenty-one. Over the years, I had watched her light dim, flicker, and go out. Her self-fulfilling prophecy came true when an unidentified assailant brutally murdered her two months before her 21st birthday.

It was challenging but I managed to locate the perfect dress. It was a pink empire-style dress with long sleeves, a high neck, and frills around the collar. Very feminine, nothing like she would wear. She was not a pink kind of girl. But I needed her outside to match her insides—soft and gentle. It didn't matter to me what impression others had of her prior to her murder. Today was going to be the last time anyone would ever see her, and I wanted her to leave them with an impression of her true essence—a gentle, loving soul.

I could not think about what her last moments of life must have been like. The terror she must have felt, the aloneness, the guilt and regret. Pushing those thoughts out of my mind, I focused on getting this dress to the mortician. I felt sad when I gave him the dress. This man knew her and cared greatly for my friend. She had worked next door at the barbershop and was the mortuary's official barber. No barber wanted to cut the corpse's hair, but she did. She told me they deserved to look good. Now it was up to him and I to do our best to make her look good.

When I asked to see her body, he was visibly shaken. "I have never seen a corpse in such bad condition. Please give me time to work on her before you view her."

Turns out the coroner's office in Atlanta, Georgia, where she was murdered, did not do their job. We had sent a check for $700.00 to cover embalming and transport, and while they waited seven days (for the check to arrive from San Francisco and then clear) before releasing her body, they kept her on ice and mailed her naked frozen body back to us instead of preparing her for burial. To them, she was just a junkie nigger whore from California who got what she deserved. It didn't matter she was someone's daughter, sister, or beloved friend.

And they weren't the only ones who appeared to feel that way. The weekend she was found, there were seven other murders in that part of town. The detectives said looking for her killer was useless. It didn't matter that somebody had beaten, strangled, and tortured her. Or that she was so severely mutilated her womb had to be removed to conduct an autopsy.

Thinking about the horrible images of my friend threw me into shock. I was angry and wanted someone to pay. But who would that be? The boyfriend who introduced her to heroin? The man who pimped her out in Atlanta? The killer who ended her young life? The father who stole her innocence? The mother who failed to protect her and get her help? Maybe I would go on a one-woman rampage against the racist police who didn't recognize her value as a human being. But my desire for retaliation wasn't an option; I just needed to keep it together and put my friend to rest.

On many occasions, we'd walked into this building together to view our friends' who had died from drugs, violence, and suicide. Today, she was the one lying in the white coffin. Looking up at the marquee, I saw her name in bold white letters. As I slowly approached the casket, my knees buckled and I forced myself to walk those extra ten feet and look down into my friend's face. All I could do was gasp in horror. Oh, my God!! Who was this person? This was not my twenty-year-old friend. She looked like a forty-year-old, middle-aged woman who had lived a hard life.

I looked inside the coffin for her glasses. Everyone called her granny because of the style of glasses she wore. She was known for them, and they were missing. This wasn't right. Her glasses needed to be here. I could see tiny pinpricks of Black all over her face. What was that? I looked at the mortician standing next to me with pleading eyes. He dropped his head and told me rigor mortis had already set in by the time she arrived. "We did the best we could in trying to cover it up."

Although they draped lace fabric over the casket, it failed to camouflage her decomposing skin. I left the mortuary, went to the fabric store, purchased a yard of thick, ornate lace fabric, and draped the new lace over the casket. Only her silhouette was visible. She now looked like a sleeping angel instead of a rotting corpse.

During the quiet hour, I was paralyzed as I knelt at the coffin of my best friend. In my mind's eye, I could see us together as six-year-old girls and then sobbed uncontrollably as the last words she said to me filled my mind.

On that fateful night, I was entertaining when she knocked on the door and asked if she could talk to me. I excused myself and went into her room. It was very dark, and I wondered what was happening. She told me she was leaving on a trip in the morning. We had been living in our house for only two weeks and I could not believe she was going away so soon and with a man who had shot her in the leg. I was horrified. Looking at me, she calmly said the last words I would ever hear her speak: "I will be back. I might be back in a box, but I will be back." Three months later, she returned just as she had predicted—in a box!

The trauma of her murder was too overwhelming for me to face. She had been my savior, protector, and motivator. Her love saved me from years of sexual molestation, and her listening ear provided a place to share those hidden secrets. After her funeral, I was lost. Anger and grief seeped into every cell of my body, leaving no room for love, joy, happiness, or life. On the outside, I looked fine. But on the inside, I was screaming for help. No one could hear me because I was standing in the Legacy of Silence. In this place I kept my pain and grief hidden away. Speaking about such things was not allowed. I was a Black woman and we lived with our pain behind a wall of silence.

The day I said goodbye to her, a part of me was buried with her. I disappeared into a Black hole of grief. My body was still here, but the essence of me was gone. I had to find a way to live with my pain. My very survival depended on it. I increased my own drug use, hoping it would numb the pain. It didn't. And so I escaped into marriage. The outspoken activist and fiery young woman silently slipped away, and no one even noticed.

Did you ever lose someone close?

How do you live with your grief?

Did you share the pain with anyone, or suffer in silence?

"We need to reshape our own perception of how we view ourselves. We have to step up as women and take the lead."

Beyonce

Part III

Rewriting Our Narrative

Claiming Our Throne

Blinded by Trauma

Black women have inherited a nurturing gene that kicks in anytime we see someone in need. It doesn't matter how old we are; that urge to protect is instinctual. But, if we can't help, a feeling of powerlessness overtakes us. After experiencing incident after incident of powerlessness, our psychic is traumatized.

Living in a racist White world, we constantly experience personal and communal pain. The horrific incidents inflicted upon our community distort how we view the world, and the lenses of innocence we once looked through are replaced and we are blinded by trauma. No longer seeing the beautiful colors of joy, happiness, and peace, we live in a world of gray tones.

We often hear individuals speaking about post-traumatic stress (PTS) and how it impacts lives. Sistahs live with PTS on two levels. First, we labor under the inherited trauma our ancestors experienced. Though it often goes unrecognized, it is so much a part of our existence that it feels normal. And then we live with Present Traumatic Stress—the trauma that originates from events occurring today.

We can only survive all that we live with because of the inherited strength and resiliency from our ancestors—the Original Queens.

When I entered my teens in the 1960s, something started happening. Black people began openly voicing what I already knew. We aren't inferior. We are capable, intelligent people that deserve equality. Malcolm X enlightened us on the oppressive nature of systemic racism. The Black Panthers taught us to stand, defend our Blackness, and support our community. Nina Simone's song "Mississippi, Goddam" spoke loudly about the atrocities occurring in the south. "I am Black and proud" became the overture for my new life.

Making a declaration of my Blackness to the world was serious for me. I didn't look at wearing my hair natural or changing my way of dressing as a fad. It was a change in consciousness— one I struggled with. Even though I knew about the Land of Black People, (the Island of Bermuda) my conditioning in this country overshadowed that knowledge. The false narrative that my hair in its natural state was ugly but long straight hair was beautiful was ingrained into my subconscious. It took work to dig it out and replace it.

Putting on a dashiki and forking my curly hair into an Afro was my first step toward personal liberation. And even though that act was liberating, I still struggled with internal anger, shame, and painful secrets.

White America reacted violently to Black Liberation efforts. As more African Americans broke the Legacy of Silence and used their voices to speak out, White America went crazy. They needed to silence our voices and restrict our actions. Us openly declaring our Blackness, moving into White communities, attending colleges, winning political offices, policing our communities, and organizing self-empowerment programs threatened their authority. They needed us to be the good negroes and stay in our place.

The White power structure started systemically eliminating anything that supported Black equality. Black leaders and activists were murdered in cold blood. Individuals like my beloved shero, Angela Davis, were falsely accused of crimes and thrown in jail. Brothers returning from the Vietnam war were denied G.I benefits after risking their lives for this country. Black laborers' livelihoods were threatened if they participated in the labor movement.

My regular experiences in Bermuda had only intensified my desire to live freely. I refused to accept the dictates of White America. I used my voice to speak out against the atrocities committed toward my community. Another blessing was the education I received in the Black Studies Department at San Francisco State University, which reinforced what I learned in Bermuda. We are strong, resilient people. I am the descendent of Queens.

Because of the resistance from White society at the time, I felt like I was trying to climb a mountain that continued to get higher. However, the lessons my professors taught about my

African heritage empowered me. I was encouraged to question the status quo and draw new conclusions about my life. As a result, I started to develop newfound independence, which became the foundation for my liberation.

The Great Uncovering

In a monastery in Thailand, there is a Buddha statue that is nine feet, eight inches tall and weights five-and-one-half tons. In 1957, the monastery was being relocated. And while attempting to move the statue, a monk noticed a large crack in the clay. When they removed an area of clay, they discovered it wasn't clay beneath but solid gold.

History has it that the Buddha had been covered in clay over 300 years ago by Siamese monks to keep it from being stolen by the invading Burmese army. But unfortunately, all the monks were killed in the invasion, and the secret about the Golden Buddha remained hidden.

Sistahs are like the golden Buddha. Our true essence was covered over, hiding our identity as the Original Queens. Living in this country, the image projected of us is not who we are. Much work has gone into deceiving us with a false narrative. It's unfortunate, but many sistahs live entire lives looking at that false reflection in the mirror, believing it is who they are. We cannot recognize the truth of who we are until that outer covering (false narrative) is removed.

Today, I feel blessed for the circumstances that led me to look beyond that false narrative. What I discovered was a Queen, ready to replace her crown and reclaim her throne.

May Duty Henry

February 8, 1820 – December 5, 2015

Mrs. May was my mom and a trailblazer who made a difference in the world. With only an eighth grade education, she raised ten children, who have each gone on to make a mark in this world. We may not have had everything we wanted, but the one thing that we did have was a mother who loved us unconditionally and was always there for us. The values she stood for were instilled within us forever.

Her unconditional love extended out beyond her immediate family. Her house was always filled with her children's friends, and they were all welcome. Her hospitality and cooking were legendary, and hers was the house to eat holiday dinner at.

Her favorite saying was, "Remember to pray about everything, and if you pray, don't worry." She had a gentleness about her and a quiet resolve. She would be proud to see her legacy being displayed in the lives of her children, grandchildren, great-grandchildren, and great-great grandchildren.

A True Queen, she is missed and loved

Deborah Duty

"Everything has an end."
African Proverb

Chapter 13

A Death

When I said my life ceased to exist after Laura died, I meant it literally. My ability to cope with life was non-existent. Her death broke me. My world split in two—pre-death and post-death. Living the same life I had shared with her was impossible, and living without her felt impossible.

The intensity of my grief was so powerful, no drug could dull my pain. I only had two objectives: leave my current life and try not to be consumed by my anger/grief. Quickly, I identified a man I barely knew and used him as my out. I told him I would marry him if we lived together for a year, even though this man had no intention of getting married. But I needed to escape my current life, and he needed to feel wanted. So, we got married.

Getting married was the perfect way to ditch my old life. I changed my name, moved out of the neighborhood, dropped out of college, and walked away from my dreams. The hope was that all of this would save me from the all-consuming grief I felt. Unfortunately, my great escape attempt failed, and I slipped into what I call "Blackout Grief."

Grief distorted my conscious reasoning so much that two years after her death I woke up in bed lying next to a man I didn't recognize. Who was this man? Then I realized he was my husband. I vaguely remembered getting married, but everything else for the last two years was one big blur.

Outside, my husband and I looked like Black Barbie and Ken. We had a beautiful house, drove new cars, had good jobs, and always looked happy in public. But when the doors closed, another scenario played out. My anger and sadness morphed into a grief so deep, I disappeared. I hid from life inside a drug and alcohol-induced coma. My husband coped by being cold, mean, vindictive, and emotionally abusive. All of our life was lived behind a wall of secrecy!

Motherhood Loss

In my desperation to be okay and make this marriage work, I decided to get pregnant. This would make everything good. My husband desperately wanted children, so we started trying. But children were not to be in either one of our futures.

I was at work when I started to feel sick and doubled over in pain. They called an ambulance that took me to the closest hospital. The doctors examined me, gave me something for the pain, said I had the stomach flu, and released me. I felt something was wrong with my body, but I trusted the doctors and returned to work.

While at work, the symptoms returned. Only this time, they were more violent. When my stomach started to expand in a matter of minutes, I told my supervisor to get me to my doctor's hospital, which was about a twenty-minute drive away. I told her to call a taxi, not an ambulance. On the way to the hospital,

I noticed that the taxi driver was staring at me through the window, and I could feel my supervisor staring at me. I had no idea that my color was changing from caramel brown to gray. I had no clue that I was going into shock because I was hemorrhaging internally.

Sitting in the back of that taxi, I felt a calmness come over me. Then, I heard a voice saying, "You will be okay. Hold on." I could barely walk when I arrived at the hospital. My doctor wasn't on duty, so the on-call doctor examined me. When he touched my stomach, my entire body was lifted from the gurney. They immediately prepared me for surgery, agreeing that it was my appendix.

When he made the small incision to remove my appendix, my whole abdomen was full of blood and he could not locate the source of the bleeding. They called my doctor, who happened to be at a party and told her she needed to rush to the hospital for emergency surgery. I lay on the table, barely existing between life and death.

When she arrived and examined my abdomen, she discovered one of my fallopian tubes had ruptured and I was hemorrhaging profusely. Miraculously, she managed to stop the bleeding and repair the second fallopian tube.

I woke up in excruciating pain with my husband, mother, father, and stepfather staring down at me. Fully aware that something was gravely wrong, I managed to say, "I am okay." With tubes down my throat and another in my nose, IVs in both my arms, and a catheter, I was far from okay!

My doctor told me that I would have gone into shock and died if I had arrived twenty minutes later and that the calm feeling

I was experiencing on the taxi ride to the hospital was my body slowly going into shock. When I voiced concern about my ability to give birth, she explained that many women have a tubal pregnancy and go on to give birth successfully because they have a second fallopian tube.

That wasn't to be my fate. Two years later, I had a second tubal pregnancy, which terminated my hopes of ever becoming a mother. I was slipping into depression when my mother shared some words of wisdom. "Every woman is not put here to have children, but that doesn't mean you still can't care for children and provide love to them."

Her sage advice opened the door for me to step into the world of nurturing children who were not my biological children, and it was the greatest gift she could have given me. She helped me to see giving birth to children did not define me as a woman.

Living a Lie

After my last attempt to save my marriage with children was gone, I had to admit my life was a lie. I had trapped us within an imaginary world, and I now needed to release us from it. I wanted to stop the charade but didn't know how, so I continued to parade around as the happily-married woman.

In the meantime, the grief, anger, and loss started to break my body down. My drug use and drinking increased. I lost weight because I was drinking alcohol instead of eating food. And then, I was diagnosed with Discoid Lupus Erthematosus.

When stressors in my life started to trigger Lupus flare-ups, I had a revelation. I was going to become gravely ill unless I completely overhauled my life. After ten years of unresolved grief, I was depressed, insecure, angry, fearful, and drug addicted. No sign of the secure, cheerful, motivated woman who worked full-time while attending college could be found. She had buried herself alive in a tomb of silence and was slowly killing herself.

And although my life depended on it, I was too afraid to leave this toxic marriage. In fact, I was also an abused woman and didn't even know it. I was under the false belief that because he didn't hit me, I was okay. But he controlled me, verbally terrorized, and emotionally beat me down. That is abuse.

I didn't have the strength to leave my marriage or the motivation to try until the day he attacked me and I fought back by putting a loaded gun in his hands and daring him to shoot me.

That day a line was crossed—a line I didn't even know existed until that moment. I could stay and run the risk of him killing me or leave and reclaim my freedom. I chose freedom and filed for divorce the next day.

The night I watched my husband walk down the steps and out of my life forever, I was relieved and overcome with grief simultaneously. I was facing another death. My marriage had died. I sat at the top of the steps with my head in my hands, crying. I cried for the emotional and physical abuse I'd suffered. I cried for the two babies I'd lost. I cried for the years I'd wasted living in an unhappy marriage. I cried for my lost hope and forgotten dreams. I cried for the loss of my voice. I cried for those who would be horrified to hear that we were not the perfect couple everyone believed we were. I cried for the adultery I'd committed to prove I was a desirable woman. I cried because my friend and confidant wasn't there to help me.

I cried because I felt all alone and didn't know what to do about it. I cried because my sorrow was another secret I had to keep.

With each tear that fell, so did one of the invisible bars that held me captive in my invisible prison. My tears watered the soil in my new garden of life.

It was time to build a new life—one not crafted from ancestral trauma or filled with personal anger and debilitating grief, but built on a foundation of hope and self-love. I had been missing in action for most of my adult life, and no one knew. I had no idea how to put my life back on track, but God knew I had to face my drug addiction before I could be truly free.

When I smoked my first marijuana joint at fifteen years old, it had felt like I had found Nirvana. This drug calmed my nervousness, dulled the pain of secrets, and allowed me to function. Although I didn't function at 100%, I performed well enough to keep anyone from noticing I wasn't okay. Being impaired by drugs had become my natural way of being, and I had no idea I had crossed the invisible line into drug addiction. I had one more death in my life to face, but this time, it would not be an ending but a beginning—a rebirth.

Have you ever had to start over?

What did you release?

What did you take with you and what did you leave behind?

Gladys 'Mickey' Bennett

December 1, 1950 - December 24, 2021

Mickey was the most caring, honest, and trustworthy sister-in-law. Being a caregiver from an early age, she had the ability to start each day (or hour) anew. Over four decades, I witnessed her lovingly provide for family and loved ones. She always showed empathy and patience, believing these were the necessary traits for a helper.

Mickey consistently invested in the young through instruction and participation. Many requested her help, hoping Aunt Mickey would take charge.

As matriarch and keeper of traditions, she was intentional about family legacy as shown by her parents. Anything old folks did or said, she wanted to hear and laugh about. Remembering was important to Mickey.

Like blue sky returning after rain, we expected she would always be there. And she is because she is now an ancestor watching over us.

Thank You, Mickey. I miss you dearly.

Cynthia Bennett, your loving sister-in-law

*"I am no longer accepting the things I can't change.
I'm changing the things I cannot accept."*
Angela Davis

Chapter 14

A Rebirth

When my marriage ended, I felt beaten down, insecure, and lost. Everything familiar was gone. I gave up my lifestyle and after I closed my family daycare business, I had a few thousand dollars and a whole lot of fear and anxiety. Afraid because I did not know what to expect from life and anxious because I was about to step into unchartered territory, I was FREE!

Living life as a single woman was foreign to me. All of my twenties I had been imprisoned within marriage and I had no idea how to navigate this world. Venturing out into the world was challenging. Something as simple as taking myself to a restaurant evoked a fear reaction. It felt terrifying to move forward, but I dared to go because coursing through my veins was the blood of my ancestors—those courageous women who persevered and stayed the course. Knowing that sustained me, I had the fortitude to pursue my dreams and create the life I deserved, so I pulled on their strength and courage and pushed on.

In the divorce, I had only asked for two things: to have my name restored and to receive alimony long enough to complete college. I saw two pathways in the future. Return to school and earn my degree or find a "good" union job. It was a no-brainer for me. Not finishing my degree had left a hole inside that needed filling, and so I registered for college.

Little did I know there were many holes that needed filling. The most significant one that required my immediate attention was the one created when Laura died. No more marriage. No more running. I had to face my pain. For ten years, I had lived in a self-induced coma of grief. It covered me like an old familiar blanket. Taking it off would expose my painful secret, and that terrified me.

I didn't know what to do, but I needed to do something symbolically to bring closure, and show the world she was missed and loved. Finally, in prayer, I received my answer.

I would organize a memorial service marking the 10th anniversary of her death. As little girls, we both attended the same church. Although I wasn't currently attending, many people in the church remembered both of us. So when I went to the church elders and asked if I could hold a memorial service in her honor, they received my idea with joy.

I purchased a bronze communion plate and chalice that would sit on the church's altar and had them engraved with her name, date of birth, and death. Her family, our friends, and church members attended a celebration of her life. At the service, individuals spoke about her life and what she represented. The minister prayed over the items and dedicated them to the church. It was a moving and uplifting day.

During the service, I felt a shift within. For the first time in ten years, I didn't feel heaviness in my heart. Instead, I walked out of the church feeling brighter and lighter. I left behind the guilt I had carried for not stopping her from leaving town—the same guilt I had felt when I didn't stop Matthew from leaving the group.

Her memorial service was the start of my healing and Rebirth.

When we sold the house, I moved in with my father while I attended college. Living with him and my stepmother would be challenging. She was still competing with me for my dad's affection, but it was a sacrifice I was willing to make.

Returning to college was also terrifying, it had been ten years since I had been in school and there was wreckage from my past to clean up. After Laura died, I had just walked away, not bothering to withdraw from my classes, so those grades turned into F's. The first thing I had to do before I could enroll was clear my record. It wasn't easy because none of the old records were computerized; they were paper documents filled away in storage. I had to request they be found and copied.

Once I'd dealt with the wreckage, I walked onto San Francisco State University campus, looked up at the Tower, and made a commitment that I would be successful this time. Nothing was going to stand in the way of me graduating from college. It was challenging and scary, and I put one foot in front of the other. I had to learn how to study again and face the fear of being one of the oldest students in the class.

One night, as I was berating myself mercilessly for not understanding the lessons, I heard a small voice say to me, "If you keep telling yourself you can't do it, you won't." I realized my success depended on me. I was capable. I just needed to apply myself. Turning my thoughts around, I started to look at my years away from school as an asset. I had life experience—something the younger students didn't have. When I did share practical knowledge, the other students appreciated my contribution.

My confidence increased alongside my academic performance, and I graduated Summa Cum Laude in three years. Yet, on graduation day, I felt confused instead of joyful. My major accomplishment had not fixed me. That hole within me was still there.

On the outside, I looked successful. Unfortunately, on the inside, I still felt like a failure and now a fraud. That secret I'd kept hidden for twenty-two years was still there. I had managed to get through school and land a good job but, still in the throes of addiction and overwhelmed by depression, I was not 100% functional. I hid it well because that is what strong Black women do.

Through a series of events, I was appointed the director of the drug and alcohol prevention program for all elementary schools in San Francisco while I was still drinking and using drugs. Who says God doesn't have a sense of humor! God understood where I needed to go and guided me into a narcotics anonymous meeting.

I went into that meeting seeking resources to help people while still blind to the fact I was the one who needed help. My eyes were open, and my denial fell away as I listened to the description of an addict. They were not weak people with no self-will or discipline but people whose lives were controlled by drugs because they suffered from a disease. At that moment, a new door opened for me—a door that I didn't even know was right there in front of me. The door marked recovery. I walked out of that meeting and out of denial. I was suffering from the disease of addiction.

With God's and other recovering addicts' help, I stepped through that door into a new drug-free life. I will not say it was easy because it wasn't. At the time, I was in the first year of the MSW program at San Francisco State University. Some suggested I take a leave from school and focus on my recovery, but I was afraid that if I dropped out, I would never complete the program. I decided to continue my education but make my recovery a priority.

When I met with my professors and explained my situation, they were very supportive. Whenever the urge to use hit me, I would head to a meeting, even if it was in the middle of class. The beauty of N.A. is that an addict can walk into any meeting, feel at home, and hear a message of recovery—a message that would help them not use at that moment.

During that first year, I went to meetings wherever I could find one. Sometimes I was in meetings with all-White gay men, lesbians, or bikers. And I was accepted with open arms. We all had one thing in common—the disease of addiction. Because I was diligent in my recovery and schoolwork, I completed the final year of my MSW degree and my first year in recovery. Along with learning to study clean and sober, I learned how to live without using mind-altering substances.

Because a person's development is arrested at the age they become addicted, when I entered recovery at thirty four years old, my emotional development was that of a sixteen year old. And I had to re-learn all the things I learned while under the influence, including how to socialize with people, work, interact with my family, and have intimate relationships, all without using a mood-altering substance.

For the first time in my adult life, I started to feel the pain from the secrets I had kept hidden away. The unexpected death of my older sister, Almyra, provoked another avalanche of pain. Growing up, Almyra and I had grown close. I'd spent summers with her and my nieces in Bermuda. She was my big sister, and I loved her, even though she lived 3,000 miles away.

One summer, after she had moved in with her lifelong lover, I saw him beat her. I felt helpless and could not watch what was happening to her. I decided (selfishly) it was better to disassociate myself from her rather than experience the pain of feeling powerless to help her. So, I left the Island and never returned.

I know she felt betrayed by me and when I learned of her death fifteen years later, I was devastated. That old guilt of not keeping those I loved safe resurfaced. Remembering Matthew and Laura in coffins, I felt broken again.

When I boarded the plane to Bermuda, the pain was unbearable and I decided to revert to old behaviors, dull my pain. I had taken out my money and was waiting for the flight attendant to reach me with the alcohol cart when God intervened. I fell sound asleep and the alcohol cart moved right pass me! When I landed, I found a narcotics anonymous meeting, the members of which supported me through the funeral and the painful reunion with my two grown nieces.

Having lived her entire life in the Legacy of Silence, my beloved sister had never discussed her relationship with her family in the United States with her daughters. They had no idea why their mother didn't communicate with us or why she didn't call us on her deathbed but chose to die without seeing us.

After the funeral, I broke the Legacy of Silence and disclosed all the family secrets to my grown nieces. Then I told them when they were ready to accept me in their lives, I was only a call away. I also went to my sister's grave and made amends for turning my back on her when she needed me the most. Before I left, I made a promise that her grandchildren and her great, great, grandchildren would know who she was.

It took thirteen years; but when my niece called, I answered. On that visit, I sat with her and my great-nieces and shared the history of their ancestors with them. Once again, I broke the Legacy of Silence and kept my promise to my sister.

My rebirth began in narcotics anonymous. Using the twelve-step program, I learned to access those dark places within. I gained the courage to revisit the traumatic experiences that created my pain-filled secrets. I didn't want to. But if I wanted to live a drug free life, I had to. I also learned to trust women enough to share my secrets.

I had to release the anger and guilt I was hanging onto in order to heal my pain. In recovery, I discovered the one thing which could heal the pain and fill the holes (left by guilt) in my life was forgiveness. Learning to forgive myself and those I felt had wronged me was liberating. Walking hand in hand with God and my friends in N.A., I started the long journey back to the land of the living. This time I was living life with a capital "L"!

Do you keep painful secrets?

How have you dulled the pain?

How has it impacted your life?

Do you want to release those secrets?

Grace Ethel Curtis

February 2, 1912 – June 26, 1981

Grace, known to all as GayGay, was my grandmother. She was truly a lover of God and started each day reading her bible and praying. She was widowed at an early age with four children; however, her sister was ill, so she took in her three children as well and never remarried. She moved to California when her oldest son was stationed at Atwater Airforce Base near Merced, California, her adult children followed.

GayGay was such a joy to be around. She had a caring heart and was always willing to feed anyone in need. Whenever someone transitioned, she would take a homemade pie or cake to their home. She was an excellent cook. She loved beautiful hats and always had a beautiful home.

She felt it important that we knew and practiced good manners. She was a faithful member of her church and made sure we all knew about God. She felt that having a relationship with Him and good character were important to God. She was extremely friendly and had a host of friends. She always wanted what was best for me and encouraged me to get my education and treat others well. She said, "Kindness changes lives."

She will forever be remembered for her pillar of strength, kindness, her willingness to help anyone, and her love for her family and God.

Amanda L. Moore

"Not to know is bad; not to wish to know is worse."
African Proverb

Chapter 15

Life as Possibility

In recovery, I started to speak about the secrets I'd guarded all my life. I reunited with my hurt little girl and started to help her heal. I forgave my setpfather and learned how to coexist with him. I stepped into a place of forgiveness and learned how to look into personal stories before condemning individuals. As a result, I became empathetic.

I learned that everyone is living their life according to personal conditioning. When they hurt others, they are trying to satisfy an inward need that has nothing to do with the other person. Unfortunately, the other person is in the wrong place at the right time.

Mr. Grier was acting out past trauma and childhood conditioning in his behavior. He was the youngest of three children and his father isolated him from his siblings and made him feel superior to them. As a result, he was raised as a loner, believing he was better than other Black people and could do whatever he wanted without consequences.

As a young man, he got involved with a White woman, which was a death sentence in those days. She bore his child and when that union became public, he fled town to save his life. He never saw his child, but he had a deep yearning to love a child.

When he married my mother, he brought all his pain. Pain that caused him to want to love me inappropriately. When I told him I forgave him for his actions, he cried. My mother later told me he did apologize to me after the incident. I was walking away from him and didn't hear the apology. I couldn't believe I'd lived all those years not knowing he had remorse for what he had done and had apologized for it.

It was so unfortunate, but the Legacy of Silence prevented us from sitting down as a family and discussing what happened. That behavior was not in our conditioning. We didn't know how to heal together. That concept was foreign to us. Thanks to the narcotics anonymous program, I learned it was okay to break the Legacy of Silence and build a new life free of secrets and addiction.

The longer I was in recovery, the better my life felt and the more empowered I was. I had a great position as a professional social worker, doing what I had always wanted to do— serving others. I had developed healthy relationships with women in narcotics anonymous. And we openly shared our deepest darkest traumas and healed together. But I still felt like something was missing. Life was full and yet empty at the same time.

One evening, I confided to a friend that I felt guilty for not feeling happy because life was good and I didn't want to appear ungrateful for all my blessings. But I felt life had more to offer.

He invited me to attend a gathering of individuals to hear about a new way of living. I trusted my friend and followed him to a meeting with a large group of White people smiling and being friendly, which immediately made me suspicious.

I listened as the facilitator talked about living life from a possibility. I didn't quite understand what that meant. I heard her say she had always wanted to skydive, but fear stopped her. After this program, she had stepped through her fear and jumped. This intrigued me. I wanted to live freely and thoroughly and not allow my fears to stop me, but I didn't know how.

This group of people appeared to be engaged in a program that helped them step out of their comfort zone into a bigger world and live life, not from just what they knew but from a possibility.

I registered for the Landmark Forum, and in three days, I had the opportunity to take a different look at my new drug-free life. My life was limitless, but I had made up stories that limited my options. I discovered I could now create a new story—a different story. I could create the possibility of having something happen and then step into that possibility and have it occur. In this new way of living, the Legacy of Silence didn't quiet my voice. I was free to be me, and this me could be and do what I desired. This was FREEDOM!

After the forum, I enrolled in an eight-week seminar. One night a gentleman announced that President Nelson Mandela was traveling to the United States to receive the Hunger Award. A group was going to Washington, D.C., and if anyone wanted to go, to meet with them after the seminar. My hand immediately shot up. I heard myself saying I want to go; however, my internal voice said, "Are you crazy? You can't go to something like that."

I met with the group and got the details of the trip. The event was a $ 500-a-plate dinner, and the money benefitted the Hunger program. In addition, there was an F.B.I. security check for all attending. Our details needed to be submitted immediately to receive clearance before the dinner in three weeks. On the ride home that night, I had a major internal battle with myself.

My mind gave me several practical reasons why I couldn't go. I didn't have an extra $500 lying around. I had no vacation hours to take time off from work. And where would I stay if I did manage to get there? How was I going to get to D.C.? In the forum, I realized my life had unlimited possibilities. Realizing I could excel to new heights of achievement, I stopped listening to the excellent reasons my mind threw up as obstacles to prevent me from seeing my hero President Nelson Mandela. Despite outward appearances, I was going to step into this fantastic opportunity and live from possibility.

The following day, I walked into my office at the department of human services in San Francisco, and envisioning my trip to D.C., I announced to the first person I saw, I'm going to see President Nelson Mandela in Washington, D.C., all I need is $500. I was not asking for any donations; I was making a declaration. The clerk got excited and said, "Wow, when I get paid, I'll give you some money." I was stunned but said, "Thanks!" I repeated my declaration the entire day to other co-workers. Within three days, I received $500 in donations. Then I went to the director and asked if I could represent the City and County of San Francisco Department of Human Services at the affair. He agreed and donated $125 towards my trip!

Somewhere during my pronouncements, the internal conversation switched from discouragement to encouragement. I still had a long way to go before traveling to D.C.. I needed time off from work, a place to stay, and a way to get there.

First, my supervisor checked the books and discovered I did have ample comp time to cover the time off. All I needed to do was earn it before I left. This would be our secret. Then I started thinking about a place to stay and remembered the Department chair of social work at Howard University had extended an invitation to stay at the Howard University Inn if any S.F.S.U. Alumni ever visited Washington, D.C.. So I contacted him and he was delighted to provide accommodations for me. The only thing left was transportation. When I explained the situation to my father, he gave me frequent flyer miles to secure a round-trip ticket. With everything in place, I was ready. The icing on the cake came the day I found a formal dress on sale for $10! WOW!! While securing all I needed for the trip, a friend in the seminar decided he wanted to accompany me. So together, we set off to see President Nelson Mandela.

The night of the dinner, we took a cab to the hotel and when the doors opened to the grand ballroom, everybody who was anybody was in attendance. Coretta Scott King, Jesse Jackson, and Andrew Young were all there to honor President Nelson Mandela. I could not believe I was standing in a room filled with dignitaries waiting to see my hero!

As I looked around the room in awe, another possibility flashed: I was going to shake the hand of my beloved hero. I told my companion, and he immediately said I was crazy and that the secret service would stop me. Ignoring him, I started plotting my strategy, watching the stage as the special guests arrived and sat down. A door opened to the side and President Clinton entered, taking his place at the podium. I kept my eyes trained on that door as I half-listened to President Clinton speak.

The door opened, and two very tall secret service men stepped into the room accompanied by President Nelson Mandela. I calculated that when President Mandela started to exit, I would walk across the room and meet him before he entered the door. I stayed ready and when President Mandela finished speaking and turned to shake hands with those on the stage, I made my move. I stood up, straightened my dress, squared my shoulders, and started walking across the room. When my friend saw me, he jumped up, grabbed his camera, and followed.

I walked up to the secret service men, smiled, and nudged my way past them. They just stood back because I looked like I should be here. I walked right up to where President Mandela was walking down the stairs. When he was in front of me, I smiled and extended my hand and he took it. In that magical moment, my dream came true. I shook the hand of President Nelson Mandela.

He immediately disappeared through the door. As I turned around and glided back across the room, my feet didn't even touch the carpeted floor. When I arrived back at the table, I put my head down and started sobbing uncontrollably. Everyone was alarmed and wanted to know what had happened. They didn't realize I had left the table to shake President Mandela's hand. I kept my head down and raised my right hand above my head. "I shook President Mandela's hand. Who wants to shake the hand that shook the hand of President Nelson Mandela?" That night, I transitioned from living a life of limitations to living a life of possibilities!

Do you live life with restrictions and limitations?

*What would you do if all the self-imposed
limitations were removed from your life?*

Do those limitations come from what you have been told?

Alberta Simms

September 28, 1907 - December 30, 1982

Alberta Simms, whom we affectionately called Grandma, was a loving and caring woman who did everything with passion. She loved her family passionately and was a devout Christian who loved her Church passionately and was proud to be a member of the AME Church Walker temple.

I had a unique bond with my grandmother. She taught me what unconditional love meant. I'm eternally grateful for that special place I held in her heart.

Grandma's excellent character allowed her to do everything with excellence. That's one of the lessons she instilled in me—how to love with excellence. From her, I received the love that said, "Everything is gonna be alright."

She was my role model of what a grandmother looks like. Because of her, I am the grandmother and great-grandmother that I am today.

I feel blessed to have had this woman's love. Grandma raised me to have strong morals and values.

Thank you, Grandma, for loving me. You are my Queen.

Sharon Jones-Nelson

"The best way to make dreams come true is to wake up."
Mae C. Jemison

Chapter 16

The Africa Trip

That event with President Nelson Mandela changed my life forever. I stopped living inside of limiting beliefs where my past dictated my future. Six months later, I stepped into another lifelong dream of visiting Africa.

I was only eight hours away from the flight, and I was in a panic. What do I take? What do I leave? I packed and unpacked until I was exhausted, and then I didn't sleep that night. When my friend arrived to pick me up, she had just as many bags, and we almost didn't have enough room in the car. But we stuffed and stuffed until we got them in, and off we went.

When we arrived at the Paris airport, we discovered we exceeded the bag requirement for our flight to Johannesburg, South Africa. We had to leave something behind. Instead of spending our layover time resting in the Paris airport, we repacked our bags. We had to purchase new suitcases and pay a $200 storage fee to leave the things we couldn't take.

Our travels in Africa were indescribable. We volunteered at the Landmark Forum in Kenya and Zimbabwe. We visited the open market in Kenya and walked through Victoria Falls in Zimbabwe. We visited orphanages in Johannesburg. Once again, I was mesmerized by a life adventure I would have never experienced had I not learned how to live life from possibility.

I never missed any of that stuff we put in storage at the Paris airport. We did, however, miss our $200. And because we had to combine what we purchased in Africa with the stuff we left in Paris, we ended up paying overweight fees to fly home. Dragging all that excess baggage along cost us $350 and a lot of stress.

Overpacking for that trip was symbolic for me. That extra stuff I tried to haul with me represented everything I used to carry around with me—guilt, hurt, anger, frustration, regret, grief, and worry. I learned that life is a beautiful, glorious trip, and I don't have to take things on my journey that don't serve me.

Living life as a possibility not only opened me up to new adventures, it opened me up to God's guidance. I didn't know it then, but my healing wasn't just for me. God had a much higher calling for me—one I could not even imagine. But I first needed to dive deeper into who I was and how I showed up in the world.

Do you carry excess baggage when you travel?

*Has that excess baggage turned into a
burden that weighs you down?*

*Is it time to clear your physical, emotional, and
mental spaces of unwanted objects?*

Iola Fountain

March 2, 1943 – May 26, 2016

Inspired by her mother's passion to say a kind word or do a kind deed to help someone on their way, Iola pursued a career in professional social work. She was promoted to management because of her grace, fairness, and leadership skills. Her staff admired the organizational culture of love and respect she created for the clients and workers.

In the community, she showed that same love and worked diligently in her church to provide outreach services. She extended advocacy work to include political organizations like the NAACP.

Opening her big heart and sharing her love Iola adopted a brother and sister. When she had grandchildren they loved her dearly.

She loved the Los Angeles Lakers and even named her beloved little dog after Kobe Bryant. Shopping was a favorite pastime. She was a fashionista who made a statement wherever she went.

Iola's moto in life was, "You got to know when to hold them and when to fold them."

Queen Iola is greatly missed by all who knew and loved her.

Your loving sister,

Matti

"The ruin of a nation begins in the homes of its people."
African Proverb

Chapter 17

"Ubuntu" | My Sistah's Pain is My Pain

In my role as an emergency response social worker, I was the first one called when an issue was identified in the home and the first to come in contact with mothers who gave birth to babies who were born addicted to drugs. During the crack cocaine epidemic, having several newborn infants in intensive care wasn't unusual for me. All were waiting to be discharged into foster care because their mother was incapable of caring for them.

I stood in yet another hospital, ready to remove another drug-exposed newborn from a crack-addicted queen who had been stripped of her power. Every time I had to remove a child from their mother, my heart broke. Even though this was my job as a child welfare worker, I knew that these mothers giving birth to drug-addicted babies didn't want this. They were caught in the grip of addiction. The welfare system I worked for made no real effort to help them.

The system would offer them drug treatment, and when they completed their treatment and were on the road to recovery, we threw them right back into the lion's den. The only place they could move with their children was straight back into the drug-infested housing projects. We all knew it would only be a matter of time before they were smoking crack again.

The workers constantly advocated for the city to create drug-free living environments for these mothers and their children, but the request fell on deaf ears. The city could easily take several public housing complexes, fix them, secure them, and move these mothers into them. Having safe housing would give them a fighting chance to stay in recovery and parent their children safely.

The workers heard the pleas of the mothers for suitable housing. We saw the drug dealers pursue the mothers when they returned home clean and sober. The workers saw their clients slowly pulled back down into the cold, brutal world of active addiction. And there wasn't a damn thing we could do to prevent it. We felt helpless all the time.

On this particular day, the hospital removal was excruciating because I had to remove this mother's newborn baby and her other two children. Three years prior, when her second child was born addicted, she signed a contract with child protective services, in which she retained custody of her two children as long as she went into treatment and agreed that if she had another child born drug-exposed, we would remove all three children from her custody. There would be no discussion or investigation—just immediate removal.

Mom had worked hard to get clean. She had completed a drug program and was preparing to move into a new apartment with her two children when the emergency housing system ran out of funds. Instead of being relocated to a drug-free environment, she returned to her old drug-infested neighborhood and ended up living with her two babies in a transient, drug-infested hotel. To make matters worse, her baby's daddy, a practicing crack addict, got out of jail and moved in with them. It was only a matter of time before she started using, became pregnant, and was back in the system.

Everything appeared routine at the hospital until the head nurse casually informed me that because they didn't want the mom to get upset and possibly cause a disturbance, the hospital social worker had not told the mother a police hold had been placed on her baby. A police hold gave the hospital the legal right to retain custody of the child. In fairness to the mother, the hospital social worker should have immediately informed her of the police hold and the fact that her baby was not going home but into foster care. But the staff didn't because they were more concerned with how the mother would react toward them than about how her momma heart would feel.

I was shocked. In this case, not giving notice of the hold was especially cruel since mom had visited her baby every day for a week and was about to lose all of her children. Having arrived with her two other children and the baby's father to take her newborn home, she had no idea what was about to happen.

I looked at the nurse. "Do you think that letting her visit her baby for a whole week was fair when you knew all the time you weren't going to let her take her daughter home? You just signed her arrest order."

I realized this situation would likely erupt into violence. It was up to me to tell her. I called for police assistance and explained the situation to the Black female and a White male officer. I told them under no circumstances were they to let her leave with a child. They were to stay by the elevator doors.

The moment she looked up, she recognized me. "What the hell is Child Protective Services doing here? My baby is fine!" Furious with the hospital staff, I remained calm. "I'm sorry. I know what I am about to say will upset you, but I have to remove your baby and other children."

She screamed at me, "I have been coming here for a whole fuckin' week and no one said shit to me! You're full of shit! CPS is always around messin' in people's lives!" She pushed past me, walked with her toddler in the stroller, and attempted to get into the elevator. The police were standing in the hallway, and I yelled at them to stop her.

The female officer moved forward, and the mom slapped her in the face. The two officers grabbed her arms, and all went sprawling on the floor. She was kicking, screaming, and trying to bite the officers while the little boy sitting in the stroller cried.

The dad was holding his son and screaming at the police not to hurt his woman. As I turned the stroller away from the two police officers and her struggling on the floor, I saw the White hospital staff peeking out of their office doors. It was their insensitivity that had created this nightmare.

The police finally subdued her, cuffing her face down on the floor with her arms behind her back. Screaming obscenities and crying, she looked up at the Black female police officer with hatred in her eyes and venom in her voice. "You Black bitch! You are going to help this White motherfucker take a sistah down?!" Then she looked at me and screamed, "You fuckin' BABY SNATCHER! Both you bitches ain't shit, working against your own sistahs!"

The words tore into me like I'd been shot with a high-powered gun. The air left my lungs, and as I fought to breathe, the words reverberated in my head, "BABY SNATCHER! BABY SNATCHER!" My vision blurred and everything around me moved in slow motion. She was face down on the floor, the officers fighting to stand her up. The baby boy was still in the stroller crying while the dad holding his baby son screamed at the police.

I put my head down in shame.

When I arrived back at the office, I was tired, angry, and sad. The anger was for the racist hospital staff that didn't dare to face a difficult situation and be upfront and honest with this Black mom. I was sad because she had identified the Black female police officer and me as the enemy. I was tired because it felt like no matter what I did, it didn't help. I was working within a system that wasn't designed for me to help those in need. Instead, it was robbing Black women of their power. The false narrative that Black people could not create loving, nurturing family environments were used to justify why Black children represented 95% of the children in the system when Blacks were only 12% of San Francisco's population.

I could not keep doing this job because I contributed to the problem. As a child welfare worker, I was helping a racist system destroy Black families. My heart hurt, and I was filled with guilt and remorse. I had to get out before I lost my humanity and damaged more Black families in the guise of helping them.

Deep in my heart, I knew the false narrative was untrue and did not represent us. But I needed to answer the question, who are we? There was only one place where I would find my answers, the motherland. And that is where I had to go. I didn't know when or how it would happen, but I didn't need to. God was guiding me.

Have you experienced feeling another Black woman's pain?

Were you a contributing factor in her pain?

Has pain forced you to make drastic life decisions?

Saundra Allen

July 19, 1963 - March 10, 2010

SGT. Saundra Renee Allen was a devoted wife, loving mother, and US Army Veteran who served her country both overseas (Korea) and Stateside (Ft. Hood, TX).

Saundra raised two beautiful children, Brandon Pierre Allen and Tia Joy Allen, both successful in their own right. Brandon, an accomplished singer and recording artist, and Tia, an educator.

Saundra was rooted in her faith as a Christian and a deaconess in her church, New Beginnings Community Outreach Church. Grounded in her calling to be of service to life and mankind, Saundra obtained her BSN from North Carolina A&T State University School of Nursing in Greensboro, NC. She became a Registered Nurse (RN). She was a proud "Aggie," filled with "Aggie Pride."

Saundra lived her life like it was golden and loved giving back to the community. When she developed Stage 4 Breast Cancer, Saundra continued to look after her patients (who also had cancer).

Saundra was a mighty warrior of God and fought a good fight. Saundra left this world better than she found it. She blessed everyone she encountered. We are all better for knowing this powerful Queen.

Jamal Bey

"It is better to travel alone than with a bad companion."
African Proverb

Chapter 18

The Spiritual Healer

Sometimes to know who we are, we have to break out of the illusion of who we believe ourselves to be. To break out, we first need to break open. Pain can be very effective in breaking us open. I experienced a pain so intense, I had to lean on Spirit for support. That is when I found my true purpose as a Spiritual Healer.

The Code Breaker

Sistahs come from a legacy where we weren't allowed to call anything our own. We were the property of another. And as a result, we could lay claim to nothing. But sometimes, we were allowed the privilege to have a relationship with a man. Even though that man might be with another, we knew he was no one else's. We had the legitimate right to claim him and he us.

There was a code between Black women. We didn't share our men. I didn't sleep with your man, and you didn't sleep with my man. I don't care how broken down or "trifling" we thought he was. And if you were my friend, you didn't flirt with him. If he tried to sneak up on you, you would simply turn around and say, "Do you want me to tell my girl that you are trying to slip up on me?" We honored that code, and we lived by it. No one wanted to be labeled a code breaker!

My mother did not compromise when it came to upholding the code. I remember waking up one day and being told my best friend's house was off limits. Mom was very clear, "You can't go over there anymore." And overnight, I lost a family I had been with from birth. My play cousins no longer existed for me. In my household, you did not ask the question, "Why?" You just accepted the facts that adults put in front of you.

During the last nine months of my mom's life, I mustered the courage to ask her why she stopped hanging out with her best friend and she answered, "Because she was sleeping with our other friend's husband. And as Black women, we don't do that to each other. We have too much stuff to deal with without our girlfriends' betrayals. We must hold our love for each other sacred. And so, I ended my friendship with her. I could not look our other friend in the eye, knowing that she was being stabbed in the back. I am not that type of woman."

Although she didn't use the word the code, I understood what she meant. My girlfriends also received the code from their mothers. The code bonded us together as sistahs. It created a foundation for that safe place we all needed to have, especially with all that Black women face. Breaking the code means you could crush your sistahs and cause her a pain she might never recover from. So, no matter how much you liked him or he liked you, you maintained the code.

Unfortunately, some sistahs break the code and hurt others when they are dealing with their pain. They don't see the consequences of their actions.

The Betrayal

I was lying in bed, covers pulled over my head because I was trying to hide from the world. I didn't want to come out. I was in excruciating pain. My heart ached and I could barely breathe. I couldn't believe it. Not only did she break the code with me, but she also broke it with the sistahs in our women's group that we co-facilitated.

Our group was focused on empowerment and holding each other up. We all had trust issues, and I had created the group to build sisterhood. I couldn't believe she had sat right next to me in a previous group discussion about sistahs betraying each other, and all the time she was sleeping with my man.

The phone rang, and I answered it even though I didn't want to. She called to ask when we would resume the woman's group. I bolted upright in the bed, and that thing in the middle of my stomach exploded! "Are you fucking crazy? I wouldn't be in the same room as you because I don't trust you as far as I can spit. You betrayed me and destroyed everything I was working to establish with the group."

What I said about betrayal didn't seem to register with her. In fact, she had the nerve to tell me that women always get mad at each other and never get angry at the man. We let him off the hook. I regained some composure as I reminded her that I held *her* responsible for her behavior. I did not hold him accountable for what she did. She chose to pursue him and be sexually involved with him and ignore the facts that her husband was his best friend and she was co-facilitating a woman's empowerment group with me. I told her never to call my house again and hung up. She had betrayed the sistahood. She was a code breaker.

Left to deal with the consequences of her actions, I had to figure out how to disclose this level of betrayal to the sistahs in the group. They trusted me and depended on me to create a safe space. That was my promise to them, one which had been broken. Unfortunately, the group did not survive the betrayal.

The sistahs in the group expressed hurt, frustration, and anger. They blamed me for convincing them to trust us. Somehow, it was my fault that they once again had experienced betrayal after trusting a sistah, even though they pointed out that I was a victim also. This situation confirmed their earlier conclusions about Black women. They can't be trusted. I could not convince them to continue the group and they left with the bitter taste of betrayal on their lips.

She broke our hearts. There was no way for me to alleviate their pain or mine. She chose to make herself feel good at the expense of other sistahs who were trying desperately to heal from their pain. I did recognize her pain. I even understood it. However, it did not excuse her behavior or hurt me any less. I had to find a way to deal with the pain of being betrayed by another Black woman and the pain my sistahs felt because I failed to protect them. This was on top of the pain of having the man I loved leave me for another woman.

Have you ever been betrayed by a sistah?

How did you deal with the pain?

Did you keep silent or share your feelings with someone?

The Voice Within

My pain was debilitating. Yes, he betrayed me and she betrayed me. But what hurt the most was that I had allowed it to happen. I genuinely believed that I could keep others from doing behaviors that would hurt me. But the truth was what they did had nothing to do with me. They were engaging in actions to make themselves hurt less. I wasn't even a consideration. Not understanding that at the time, I blamed myself. I probably felt the same way my mother did when my father betrayed her.

My life became challenging because we traveled in the same circles. I was in recovery, and so were they. I would see one of them every single day because I could not run away from attending narcotics anonymous meetings. N.A. is where I went to deal with life without using drugs and alcohol. This was a significant dilemma. My old coping mechanisms were not available and in order to face my pain in a healthy way, I had to expose myself to them.

I needed an outlet for my pain, or it would consume me. I was also terrified my anger would cause me to hurt someone, especially since I was choosing not to numb the anger with substances. I had to pull myself up out of this dark hole. I wanted my joy back.

Every day after work, I would drive to a local lake and walk the five miles around it. I put all my energy into walking to dissipate the pain in my heart and quiet the thoughts running through my head. "He loves her because she is better than you are. You were stupid to trust them. All your friends are looking at you and laughing. They are happy and you are alone and sad."

As I walked, I'd look up at the big, beautiful trees and for one hour, it was quiet and peaceful inside my head. Sometimes, when I looked at these mighty eucalyptus trees, it felt like they were talking to me. Of course, I would dismiss it as being stupid. They were trees and didn't talk. But one day, I heard an unfamiliar voice speaking to me. Even though it was in my head, it didn't sound like my voice. It sounded like another voice, but I couldn't identify whose it was.

"I'm going to tell you a story."

I accepted it as my active imagination and a way of addressing that internal pain. Every day, this voice would tell me stories as I walked and I would listen and be amused. Sometimes I wondered if this was the beginning of me losing my mind. But nobody knew what was going on in my head, so I was safe.

In my world, you got called crazy when the thoughts in your head spilled out into the world and others started hearing them. So if I acted normal and sounded normal (even though I was going crazy on the inside), I would be fine.

One day, the voice said, "I want to tell you something." Used to the voice telling me stories, I listened. "There's a spirit that lives inside of you, and its name is Ahmondra. Ahmondra is a powerful spirit that will facilitate healing on the planet. You are not to share that name with anyone." Each day, I learned more and more about Ahmondra , the spirit within me.

I listened in silence for three years, never revealing my internal conversations or Ahmondra's identity to anyone.

Then one day, while sitting with a good friend who is a prophet, the voice told me to share my story about Ahmondra with him. He listened and told me, I would know when to reveal Ahmondra's identity to the world. I was not to worry about it. I'd receive a sign when the time was right.

The Healer Revealed

Not long after our conversation, my friend and I attended a sizable transformational conference in Atlanta, Georgia. The conference, The Black Summit, was organized by African Americans who had completed the Landmark Forum. Once a year Landmark graduates came together and discussed personal transformation from an African American perspective.

On the second day of the conference, I went to the microphone and shared how I had hidden a drug addiction for most of my life. I was in the middle of sharing how I had graduated from college and held down full-time professional jobs all while using when the head moderator interrupted.

"Did you hear what you just said?"

I stood there, puzzled and dumbfounded. I had no idea what he meant. He went on to say he used drugs most of his life and yet couldn't accomplish anything. He finished with, "You're standing here in front of us, saying that for twenty-two years, you were in the throes of your addiction and had significant accomplishments. I'm jealous. Do you realize what other greatness you could have accomplished if you were not addicted to drugs? Do you realize how great you are that you could do all you did with that significant handicap?" I was stunned. "You are an amazing individual, and you must recognize and celebrate that!"

At that moment, my whole life flashed in front of me. I saw the times I had struggled just to function. The moments I'd wrestled with acute anger, rage, self-doubt, and depression, but gotten up and went out into the world anyway. The days I pushed my feelings deep inside after an assault on my character by the larger society. The days I wearily put on extra makeup to hide the dark circles under my eyes from the sleepless nights. Overwhelmed by my realization of who I was and what I had accomplished, I broke down crying.

No one had ever helped me look at myself from that perspective. What started as crying dissolved into uncontrollable sobbing. The sobs rose from the depths of my soul, and I could not stop them. My whole body started to shake. As I closed my eyes, I felt the warm embrace of loving arms around my body. Someone was hugging me.

All I could do was stand there crying. I had no idea what was happening around me—that women had left their seats to join the group hug growing around me. I didn't know everything in the room had stopped. The moderators had ended the whole session, and those men and other women who hadn't joined this massive circle around me had stood up and lined the conference room's walls. I was standing in the center of a circle of fifty women.

Something started happening inside my body. Waves of emotions rushed up to the surface from deep within my soul. Then I heard the voice. "Push out energy." I had no idea what that meant, so I focused my attention on my internal energy and began pushing. I pushed from within and pushed and pushed until I had nothing left within. I was completely drained with a feeling of resounding peacefulness.

The arms slowly began to loosen from around me. When they were all gone, someone helped me to a chair. Sitting with my head down and my eyes closed I wondered what had happened. I heard my good friend, the prophet whispering in my ear, "Now is the time to introduce the world to Ahmondra. Please go and have them change the name on your name tag." I went and had my name tag changed from Brenda to Ahmondra.

A woman known as a powerful Spiritual Healer in the community came up, looked deeply into my eyes, and asked me to place my hands on her side and send healing energy to it. "You are a Healer now. Step into your power." Although I didn't understand, I did what she said.

In my mind, I was shouting, "What do you mean? I am a Spiritual Healer? That's you, not me. I don't even go to church. I don't even know what relationship I have with God."

She must have seen my confusion and doubt because she took my hands and made a declaration. "You are a powerful Spiritual Healer. Own it!" She told me not to worry about what I didn't know—that I only needed to believe that God would guide me and help me come into the fullness of my healing power.

Later that evening, as I walked around in a daze, still trying to comprehend what had happened, people hugged me and told me that today was magnificent. I had no idea what they were talking about. Then, a sistah approached me. "Sistah, I don't know what you did, but you healed me. When I came to this workshop, I had been bleeding for months, and no doctor could tell me what was wrong. As I stood in that circle, heat radiated out from the center where you were standing. The entire circle of sistahs heated up."

"What circle?" I asked.

"No one has told you what happened? Fifty women had formed a hugging circle around you when a massive surge of heat flowed out from you and the entire circle got hot. When I left that circle and went up to my room, the bleeding had stopped. My beloved sistah, you healed me!"

Hearing her testimony sent me into a panic. In my mind's eye, all I could see was the woman who had touched the hem of Jesus's garment and received healing. Oh my God! This woman was saying I had the same healing powers as Jesus. I was terrified. Who was I to be compared to the master, Jesus?

The next day, a group of us went to the mall and saw a kiosk where you could find out the true meaning of your name. You type your name into a computer, and it provides a list of characteristics of what your name means. I reluctantly typed in the name, AHMONDRA. When the definition appeared— "Spiritual Healer"—I felt faint. This was the exact title the healer had given me the night before. I was a Spiritual Healer, and my name was Ahmondra.

Now I was left with another question: Who was Brenda? And how was she related to this healer, Ahmondra? And what was she to do with this new information?

The voice within stopped telling me stories and started guiding me. It was difficult to accept this notion of being a Spiritual Healer. As an educated woman who had trouble reconciling superstition and myth with reality, I made a silent declaration, "I will only believe when I have hard proof."

God said, "Okay. You will receive proof. And you will keep getting evidence until you completely believe and step into the fullness of who you are, Ahmondra, the Spiritual Healer."

Thus began my work of embracing myself as a Spiritual Healer. To step into the fullness of who I am, God was going to send me on a journey of healing.

Do you believe a Divine purpose awaits you?

Are you willing to embrace it?

Do you share your unique gift with the world?

Evie Lyons Bates

December 27, 1903 - January 21, 1990

My grandmother Evie was born in Branch, Louisiana, and lost her mother, Philemon Lyons, at a very young age. Grandmother was one of the oldest of her nine siblings. Two of her older sister's passed, leaving young children. Grandma and her husband moved next door to her brother-in-laws so she could help raise those children.

During the depression, her father sent food from his farm in Louisiana to his seven daughters and their families in Beaumont. Grandmother would have my mother give food to the neighbors and tell her, "Don't let your daddy see you." Grandma also purchased bags of 5 and 10 cent shirts and pants from thrift stores, distributing them to her nieces and nephews. The family thought of her as an angel.

Although grandmother had the qualities of an angel, her husband was the complete opposite. So much so that at their 60th wedding anniversary when everyone was happy and excited about their accomplishment, she looked up and said, " I don't know why y'all so happy. I been in here with the devil for sixty years. Otis been a devil for sixty years."

My grandmother was a special lady and understood the importance of legacy.

When she shared life stories with me, I knew she was courageously breaking a silence she had held for sixty years. She wanted me to benefit from the knowledge she had learned over her lifetime. For that, I am forever grateful. Thank you, Grandma. You are my Queen.

Gloria Pitre Young Thomas
ACSW-MSW

"Everybody has a calling. And your real job in life is to figure out as soon as possible what that is, who you were meant to be, and to begin to honor that in the best way possible for yourself."
Oprah Winfrey

Chapter 19

The Healing Journey

A year after my experience in Atlanta, I had an opportunity to travel to Zimbabwe, South Africa. I would chaperone a group of twenty-three students from San Francisco State University on an educational tour. Excited to travel to Africa again, I had no idea God was at work, planning to give me the proof I needed to accept my role as a Spiritual Healer named Ahmondra.

I knew intuitively that I would find some answers in Africa but had no idea how I would see these answers.

When we arrived in Zimbabwe, we spent time learning about the culture at the University of Zimbabwe and how this country went from being called Rhodesia, run by Whites, to Zimbabwe, run by Blacks. Then we took a week-long road trip into the countryside, or what they call the bush.

Traveling from village to village, we experienced so much culture and I experienced a series of proofs.

In the first village, we went into a hut to meet with a traditional healer or Inyanga. This traditional diviner used the throwing of bones to assess what was occurring within an individual, and then they offered a remedy.

About twenty of us filed into the hut and sat in a circle. The Inyanga held the bones in his hands, spoke words over them, and threw them on the floor. Then he moved around the circle and started revealing who we were and what was going on with each of us. When he got to me, he looked serious. "You have strong powers. You are a healer."

I looked over at my girlfriend, who was also on the trip with me and laughed. "Did you tell him I want to verify I am a healer?"

"You know I do not talk to strangers, especially in Africa. I did not tell him anything about you."

In my mind, I questioned how this man could know who I was—how he could look at me and confidently declare that I was a healer. I brushed it off as a coincidence, and we all went back into the van and drove off to the next village where we met with another Inyanga.

When he got to me, he asked me if I had been to Africa before? I confirmed that I had traveled to Africa, and he told me I had returned home to receive a powerful message: "You are a healer."

This time, I was stunned. I could not believe that a second healer in a different village gave me answers to a question they didn't even know I had. The group continued its journey, and a couple of days later, we arrived at the third village and were met by two Inyangas, a mother and son wearing traditional dress. They started speaking to each other in their native tongue. The mother was speaking to the son, and they were both looking at me. Before the son took out his bones, he looked at me and said, "You are a powerful healer. You should come to Africa and study with us. You have much work to do in the world."

I jumped up, ran outside, sat down by the side of the hut, and started to cry. I could no longer deny a powerful healer called Ahmondra lived within, who would help usher in a new spiritual paradigm shift occurring in the world.

I was overwhelmed by this idea of being a healer, and wondered how this would be integrated into Brenda's life. How would this powerful Spirit that represented love coexist with Brenda, the woman filled with pain and anger? Brenda had to go through a deeper level of healing and embrace a new way of being. I would learn to allow Ahmondra to look through my eyes and view the world through spiritual lenses. So much work had to be done before Ahmondra and Brenda could co-exist.

When I returned to the U.S., I knew Ahmondra was real. But I also knew that Brenda had a lot of learning to do. First, she had to learn the spiritual ways of Ahmondra to embrace this powerful Spirit and begin the work of helping others heal in this world.

I had no idea what was getting ready to happen in my life, but I did know God was working behind the scenes to help me embrace the essence of me. My life was beginning to unfold in miraculous ways. Things that had started years before were coming to fruition.

India

One day years earlier, I had been walking in San Francisco and saw a handbill lying on the ground. Picking it up, I saw a guru named Shri Shri Ravishankar would be visiting that week. I had no idea who he was or what he stood for; I only knew I had an overwhelming urge to attend this gathering.

As I sat down in the church, I felt a powerful energy behind me and turned to see a man dressed in all white walking down the middle aisle. He resembled Jesus, or what the pictures of Jesus looked like when I grew up. He wasn't White but Indian. After that gathering, I followed him to Berkeley, California, and invited several friends to experience this powerful man where we heard him talk about his Ashram in India. I made a declaration that one day, I was going to go and visit his Ashram in India.

After returning from my trip to Zimbabwe, I was attending a wedding when I overheard a good friend share he was getting ready travel to India and visit his teacher, Shri Shri Ravi Shankar. I remembered my declaration of visiting Shri Shri and informed my friend I wanted to go with him to the Ashram. Because he was a Student of Shri Shri, we were invited to have a private audience.

I lived in the Ashram for two weeks and took classes in The Art of Living Program. The lessons I learned were astounding, but the most significant impact came the day we went to his private residence. In his presence, I was unable to speak. The energy emanating from him was so powerful, it rendered me speechless. He spoke to each of us and presented us with a unique gift. When he came to me, he picked up a small figure of the God Ganesh, put it down, looked across the room, got up, and retrieved a small ancient object.

Handing me the object, he said, "This is an ancient lamp. I am giving you this lamp because you are a light in the world. You will bring healing to individuals, and this lamp will help light your way."

Sedona, Arizona

Following God's guidance I began enrolling in classes at my church and courses at community centers. Anytime Spirit guided me to enroll in a training, I did. When I registered in a workshop called "Healing the Inner Child," I looked forward to the week-long seminar in Sedona, Arizona, on indigenous peoples' holy ground.

Once again, I found myself in an environment of revelation. The opportunity to participate in a traditional Indian sweat lodge was remarkable and introduced me to Spirits that I could see with my eyes. Sitting in the darkness of the sweat lodge, I could feel the presence of Ahmondra. An overwhelming sense of peace came over me and a feeling of completeness.

The next day, I created a ceremony for Brenda and Ahmondra to be united. Along with several of my companions, I walked a medicine wheel and upon completion of it, I felt whole. An integration had occurred within that I could not explain. I left Arizona with no more questions about the role Ahmondra and Brenda would play in this world. They were not two different entities but one. Ahmondra is the divine being having a human experience as Brenda, and Brenda has learned to allow her Divinity to emerge into the world and be a healing presence.

My trips to Zimbabwe, India, and Sedona, Arizona, confirmed who I was. I accepted the truth I was a Spiritual Healer, and now I had to learn how to express in the world as one. As always, God had plans. My spiritual education would begin, but I first had to learn about my ancestral heritage and heal my deep internal pain.

Have you received a message from God/Spirit about who you are and what you are to do?

Did you follow the guidance or run from it?

Do you believe that you are a healer?

Do you know of other women in your family who expressed as healers?

Greer Brannon Collins

June 13, 1948 – February 12, 2016

Greer Catherine Brannon Collins came into this life to express unconditional love for all. Married to the love of her life, Robert, for 47+ years, Greer was mother to two amazing daughters, grandmother to four, great-grandmother to five. Each one had a special and unique place in her life.

In her words, "My Gemini nature led me to continually explore something new and different for my life." Stepping into the adventure of life beyond her twenty-six-year career at the university, Greer focused on giving back to the community by moving out of her comfort zone. Her volunteer work included Project Open Hand, SISTER/Serenity House, and Free The Heart Ministries.

Greer embraced the spiritual teachings and principles of Science of Mind through the East Bay Church of Religious Science, Oakland, CA. Becoming reacquainted with her authentic self as a unique, one-of-a-kind, unrepeatable expression of the Divine, her studies led her to become a licensed Spiritual Practitioner.

This created the space for Greer to demonstrate unconditional love and nonjudgment by assisting others in remembering and realizing their unique self as an expression of the Divine.

You may no longer live in the physical form as Greer B. Collins, but you live in the Now, free from any yesterdays or tomorrows. You are happy, free, and complete.

Your Loving Husband, Robert Collins

"I will instruct you and show you the way to go,
I will counsel you with my eye on you."

Psalm 32:8

Chapter 20

A Home Going

It took a while, but finally I learned God's schedule is not in sync with my calendar. I received the message I would move to Africa for a year to study. So, I started preparing for my journey. In my infinite wisdom, I believed Zimbabwe would be my new home because of my meetings with the Inyangas. However, while making final preparations, I received an anonymous email from Zimbabwe, a newspaper article showing that individuals were being kidnapped and never heard from again. No note was attached to the email, but it was clear that Zimbabwe was not the place to relocate.

Although everything was ready, I put the trip on hold and continued to know that I would move to Africa. For two years, I continued to tell everyone who would listen that I was moving to Africa to study culture. Finally, it got to a point where people started to think I was only talking. My statements sounded "sketchy" to me, but I never doubted God's guidance.

One day, a good friend gave me a taped sermon of his minister's message. I loved it so much, I visited her church the following

Sunday. She spoke about an African Mystic who had visited California, and I heard the voice say, "He is your teacher." Unfortunately, he had left for Ghana and wouldn't return until the following year.

I researched him and discovered he was the leader of a spiritual organization called the Etherean Mission and those who attended his church were called Ethereans. They embraced all religions and all cultures, understanding there is no separation between individuals. As metaphysicians, they believed the universe is one whole entity, and we are all connected to God's power and presence.

He was exactly who I wanted to study with, and so I patiently waited a year for him to return from Africa.

When I met and asked Brother Ishmael Tetteh, (Ethereanlife.com) if I could travel to Africa and study with him, he only asked me one question. "Can you be humble?"

I thought for a second and replied, "yes."

He said he didn't believe an American could study under him because we are an arrogant people. I had to ask myself: Was I really ready to embark on such a life-changing journey?

I knew this was the path God had chosen for me. And yes, I was ready to return to my homeland and discover who I was. Living in America, I could never truly understand my heritage. I could read about African history in books, but I needed to experience my heritage on a cellular level. I knew our history was nonexistent in America's history books. They had created a false narrative of who we are. And because we had nothing to counter it, this became our reality.

In my previous travels to the African continent, I experienced love and acceptance. The opposite of the disenfranchisement I experienced in America. I was ready to humble myself and relocate to Ghana. I rented my newly-renovated house in Oakland, CA, to friends, and entrusted my financial affairs to another friend. I packed two suitcases and two food boxes and trusted Spirit to protect me on my journey. My time spent in Ghana would be my spiritual awakening.

When I stepped onto the plan at the San Francisco International Airport, I committed to leaving my present life behind so that I could embrace my new life. Brother Ishmael's words kept ringing in my ears. "Can you be humble?" I realized to study under him, I had to show up as a blank slate. My two college degrees would be of no use in this environment. I was a student, ready to learn.

I arrived in Ghana at night and when I stepped off the airplane, I could smell the air's freshness. Something in my Spirit started to dance as an overwhelming sense of peace met the anxiety of being in a new place. Fortunately, I walked out of the airport and into the loving hands of four individuals who greeted me. I was overcome with excitement and fear as we drove to my new home.

The following day, I met my new host family—mother, father, two daughters, son, and cousin. This was going to be my home for the next three months, and the schedule set up by Brother Ishmael was tight. It was my responsibility to travel to his office daily so I hired a driver. I would arrive every morning at 9:00 a.m. and he would give me an assignment to complete. I would work on it all day and then return home at 5:00 p.m. My interaction with him would be minimal, as he kept me at a distance. I didn't know he was testing me. He wanted to see if I was serious about studying and genuinely humbled. Would I stay committed and do what was necessary?

That first few days in Ghana, I broke out in large hives, and no one knew why. I was a little concerned because I had Discoid Lupus Erythematosus. The doctors had informed me I could never live in a hot climate, and I had just moved to live in a country on the equator. I spoke to Brother Ishmael about it, and he told me my body is intelligent. If I talked to it and explained the situation, my body would hear my voice and understand. That night, I lay in my bed and talked to my body. "I understand this is a new environment with different food and water but we are okay. There is not one thing we need to be concerned about. We are safe." The following morning every hive had disappeared. Brother Ishmael also prepared a herbal drink for me and my hives never returned.

After working for about a month with Brother Ishmael, I got frustrated because every assignment I turned in was marked up in red ink. I was treating my studies the same way I did in America. Find out what the teacher wants to hear and then give them that answer. That was not what this learning experience was about.

He instructed young students that the key to learning was to give your answers. Education had to do with taking ownership of what you were learning. It had nothing to do with the teacher. It had to do with you. I decided that I was here to learn for me, not for Brother Ishmael, and I started answering the questions he gave me from my original thoughts. I stopped thinking about what he wanted and started focusing on my truth. From that moment forward, my education took on a whole new dimension.

Have you ever had to wait on God for guidance?

Has it been difficult to follow or find your truth?

Mattie Louise Glover Fountain
May 27, 1916 – June 1, 2010

Born in Jeffersonville, Georgia Mattie moved to Pleasantville, New Jersey, with her husband James Terry Fountain where they raised six children.

A Renaissance woman ahead of her time, she was a civic leader and humanitarian. Mattie said, "If I can do anything, say a kind word, do a kind deed, or help someone on their way, then my living will not be in vain."

A prayer warrior and family matriarch, she provided love and support during challenging times. A beacon of light, she lived by her motto, "On time and in time, God will answer prayer."

While picking cotton one hot summer day in Georgia, she made the decision to create a better life. Standing in faith, she courageously took her three children and traveled from Macon, Georgia to Pleasantville, New Jersey.

An audacious businesswoman, she saw the opportunity to provide cab service to the Black community in Pleasantville, New Jersey, because white cab companies discriminated against blacks. When her beloved husband passed away, Mattie provided for her family by operating the business for over seventy years.

A true saint at Mount Pleasant Baptist Church, Mattie was a woman of great faith. The driver seat of the cab was frequently converted into her pulpit. It was often said you may get into Mattie's cab one way, but you get out transformed.

Her legacy lives on through her family and those she touched along the way.

From your loving Fountain family.

"Seeing is different from being told."
African Proverb

Chapter 21

Understanding The African Heart

Brother Ishmael understood I had ancestral pain and pain from living in an angry racist society trapped in my body. To become whole, I needed to release this trapped pain. So, he took me through his program of healing called Soul Processing. In Soul Processing, I visited those deep places of pain and dissolved the emotional attachments I had formed with traumatic experiences.

On several occasions, when I went back in memory and connected with that trauma, my body discharged chemicals stored in my cells and I became ill. I felt strong physical sensations as the pain I experienced in childhood was released. The deep raging anger which lived right below the surface started to dissipate along with my PTS symptoms. As the grief energy surrounding my heart lessened, I was able to breath more deeply.

I also needed to release the ancestral pain trapped within. This called for the African way of Sankofa. Going back (in the past) to retrieve valuable knowledge that could help me in the present.

The move to Ghana was the key which opened the door to understanding my fiery anger and deep yearning. I learned to respect and appreciate the origin of my anger as a powerful energy and asset. And I recognized the yearning tugging at my heart was the familial love my ancestors left behind when they were kidnapped.

In Ghana, I was in a world where people looked like me and respected me. There was love and kindness all around and I felt no hatred, discomfort, unidentified fear, or burning anger. I walked down the streets, knowing everyone had my back. The police weren't circling the block looking for lawbreakers. Instead, there was communal pride rooted in ancestral heritage.

I woke in the morning to the sound of women singing as they swept the front yard. In the evening, I smiled at the children's laughter as they played simple games. Muslims lived side-by-side with Christians. Tribal people came to the city to be with relatives, and those living in the town opened their doors to everyone. I was amongst my people, and I felt safe for the first time in my life.

A Hole in the African Heart

One night, I sat with my friend sistah Elizabeth and listened as she told me about the impact the slave trade had on the ancestors who were left behind.

"It was painful for us because we lost our family. We would go to sleep at night, and the following day when we awoke, somebody would be gone. It was like they had just vanished into the night. A sister would be gone, a brother would be gone, a father would be gone, and we did not know where they went. Sometimes we would be in the village doing what we do every day, and someone would come running saying, 'They're coming, they're coming.' We would run and hide, but not all of us could hide fast enough. When we returned to the village, our hearts hurt because someone would be missing. We'd look for a baby brother, nephew, or niece, but they would not be found. We had no way to get them back. We lived in perpetual fear for those who remained and felt anguish for those taken. The Africans who traded their brothers and sistahs to the White colonizers were greedy, immoral, and had no idea of what they were selling their kin into. We knew slavery, but the White man's concept of slavery was foreign to us. When we conquered another tribe, the captors were incorporated into our tribe. We did not strip them of their humanity or relegate them to a lifetime of servitude."

Looking at me through tears, sistah Elizabeth spoke about the hole in the African heart. "A pain runs through every African because a piece of our heart was removed when you were taken. We lost love and connectedness when you were ripped from our arms. Our continent is a place with many holes. Holes that stunted our growth, development and disturbed our ancestors. That hole in the African heart is still waiting to be filled. We've never stopped waiting for our loved ones to return home. You are my long-lost sistah, and we love you. Your returning home fills that hole for us. You are a part of us. It's time for all of you to come back home, so we can return you to the African heart. Understand, you are not who your captors have made you believe you are."

As she spoke, I felt a quickening in my heart and a connection to my ancestral soul. We embraced each other and cried. I felt like I belonged, and she felt a healing starting within the African heart.

I visited my other friend sistah Grace and her family. Sistah Grace's mother cheered and danced when she heard that a daughter of Africa was returning from America to stay in her home. "I can die now, for my daughter has returned home, healing my African heart."

I didn't understand the full implications of me returning to Africa, as my distorted education in America had given me a false narrative of my heritage. The American history books painted Africa as a place inhabited by savages. I was taught to believe I was the descendant of uneducated, unholy people. They discouraged us from going there, pushing the false propaganda that Africans didn't like those of us who lived as enslaved people and certainly would not welcome us back. That is a lie.

Our African brothers and sistahs have never forgotten us. They have never stopped waiting for us to return home. My journey back to Mother Africa was completing a circle that was broken 400+ years ago. It was the beginning of my introduction to a state of being I had never experienced—wholeness.

In my quest to find more answers, I traveled to the central region of Ghana. I visited Elmira Castle, where my ancestors were held captive before being removed from Africa forever. It is the oldest European structure in Sub-Saharan Africa, located along the coast of Accra. I needed to see what they saw before their eyes were closed to Africa forever.

I stepped into the dark, cold dungeon of Elmina castle and closed my eyes as a rush of emotions accosted my body. There was a familiarity I could not explain. Waves and waves of memories washed into my consciousness—memories that did not belong to me. They were not vivid memories but far-off, distant memories. I could not see them in my mind's eye, but I felt them in my heart. The ghosts of my ancestors cried out to me as an overwhelming sadness engulfed me in an overwhelming feeling of déjà vu.

African women represented 30% of those kidnapped from the continent. Young mothers, daughters, sistahs, and wives experienced the trauma of seeing their loved ones placed in chains and taken away. The trauma of being removed from their communities was unbearable, terrifying, and caused many to lose sanity.

Their kidnappers often marched them long distances from their homes to the shoreline. Upon arrival at the castle, women were separated from men. There they stayed sometimes up to three months, no attention given to their personal needs. I could only imagine the shame they felt when their menses started and they could not take care of their hygiene. I hated to think of the pain experienced by a breastfeeding mother who was snatched from her infant child, or a pregnant woman realizing she would not be in the comfort of her family when she delivered her baby.

At the castle, the females' holding area was located right below the White commander's living quarters. Each night, he walked onto his balcony, looked down, and identified the woman he wanted to rape that night. His captives were helpless and endured the nightly violations silently. Huddled together in the dark and cold, I know my ancestors tried to comfort each other.

A smaller holding cell with a single small door located on the castle's coastal side was not far from the woman's dungeon. This was "The Door of No Return." Through this tiny door, the kidnapped were lowered, single file onto boats like cargo, and transferred onto larger slave ships anchored further out at sea. Staring at "The Door of No Return," my heart wept for those who had stepped through, into a new foreign world filled with unimaginable horror.

When my ancestors boarded those slave ships, their fate was sealed. The life they knew was over. They would never set foot on their home soil again, never know freedom, and never be connected to their history. Instead, they would become a new race of people (filled with memories of lost Queendoms and unrelenting anger) known as African Americans.

Those who survived the journey through the Middle Passage arrived in a world where their existence would be filled with indignities until they escaped or died. They were sold as property and endured hardships beyond imagination. Women were valuable commodities to plantation owners. African-Women possessed many skill sets. Not only was their body valuable (because of their childbearing capacity), they were skilled in basket weaving, midwifery, nursing, cooking, planting, and management. They could be rented out for additional income making them a rich commodity.

They were also used as nannies that reared generations of White children. A lactating mother would be forced to leave her baby and suckle the baby of her captors, and that same baby would one day become her owner and or torturer. This was the fate of my kidnapped ancestors.

Standing at the top of Elmina Castle and looking out over the Sea, I thought about everything my female ancestors lost, and I was filled with anger and pride. I was angry because she was held in captivity for 200+ years. That bondage took her freedom, robbed her of experiencing the lasting love of a man, enjoying the wonders of motherhood, and living as the Queen she was.

I was proud because although my sistahs were enslaved, they not only survived, but they also thrived. The chains that bound them also strengthened their resolve, enabling them to do whatever it took to live. They wore those physical chains and bore the emotional pain while loving and caring for others triumphantly.

Those amazing women hoped and prayed, while listening for whispers in the night or echoes of far-off drums, signaling that someone was on their way to freedom. Even though her physical eyes did not see freedom, her spiritual eyes did. My ancestor held onto the dream those chains would be broken one day. She would not be free, but her descendants would see freedom. So, with sheer determination, she stayed in action, blazing a trail for me to follow.

*Have you felt a yearning to know more
about who we are as a people?*

Does wearing the title of Queen feel right in your soul?

Ritual – The Lost Connection

Understanding my history also introduced me to the power underlying African culture—ritual. It is through ritual we connect to our heritage. Ceremonies within rituals anchor the culture and uphold it. They also bring order to the culture. Order gives identity to those in the family, along with protection and safety. Everyone understands and knows where they belong in the scheme of the community. I learned the importance of ancestors and how to honor them. My ancestors are part of me—a part that makes me who I am.

In Ghana, a major celebration is held in the tenth year of someone who has who passed from this life. We remember those who went before us and hold sacred all accumulated wisdom and knowledge. Keeping that close connection to ancestors creates a bond between the past, present, and future. And the ancestors are called upon for wisdom. In fact, many houses have a room used explicitly by the elder to commune with their ancestors. In the room is a stool the elder sits upon to contemplate when significant decisions are required. This stool holds all the wisdom passed down from generations of consultations with the ancestors. When the elder emerges from the room, the ancestors have revealed the answer. When that individual passes on, the next eldest person in the family steps into that role.

Rituals also help establish the critical relationship between individuals. No person ever feels alone, unwanted, or discarded. All Ghanaian newborns are celebrated with an Outdooring Ceremony. The child receives the family and community's blessing as they begin a new life. No matter how poor or rich the family is or how many children the parents have, every baby is celebrated this way. It is called an Outdooring Ceremony because Ghanaians believe that a baby remains attached to the spirit world for the first seven days of life. During these seven days, the mother and child bond and the child slowly joins the human family in the loving protection of their mother.

The Outdooring Ceremony connects the child to the community and creates a sense of wholeness and well-being within this tiny soul. The ritual begins before sunrise. The father travels with the baby to a designated location without the mother. This is the father's sacred time to introduce his child to the family. The mother will join them later when the entire community comes together in celebration.

The morning ceremony is very sacred and only attended by a close-knit of individuals. The father and his family members, the mother's family members, the designated protectors of the child (Godparents) from both sides of the family, the special invited guest, and the designated officiate or emcee (this is usually someone hired to speak at the ceremony).

The emcee announces the ancestors' names from the father's and mother's sides of the family. Next, he tells the history of each family. Then a dab of water is put into the child's mouth followed by a dab of clear alcohol. This teaches the child to distinguish between water and the bitterness of alcohol. The baby is then unclothed and placed for a few moments on the ground, so they know the feeling of the earth. Finally, the father holds the baby up and shares the child's name for the first time. When the ceremony is complete, everyone leaves in a procession to the community celebration. Here the mother, father, and baby are presented together for the first time to the community for all to see and congratulate.

The African proverb, "it takes a village to raise a child," is not just a nice phrase but an established practice in Ghanaian society. No child is ever orphaned and there is no formal government child welfare system because there is no need for one. Someone connected to them will step in and claim them no matter the circumstances, and there is no stigma on a woman and a man having a child out of wedlock in African culture. No child ever wears the title of bastard.

In one family I lived with, a niece became pregnant by her boyfriend. Her aunt and a close family friend visited the young man's home and shared the news with his mother. The mother listened and told them she would get back to them. When we left, they explained that the mother knew her son had impregnated their niece, and what I had witnessed was a formal ritual they went through in preparation for the birth of a child.

If the son accepted the child, his father and uncles would visit their home and bring a bottle of alcohol to celebrate the families uniting. If the young man's family did not return, the message was clear—he did not claim this child. For the young woman's family, that was perfectly fine because her family already claimed this child. All children were seen as blessings. The status of their parents was never an issue.

In Ghana, I was recognized as the African daughter who had returned home, and the community embraced me. Living with Brother Ishmael and the congregation of The Etherean Mission, I was immersed in the culture and learned who I was as a Black woman from the African Diaspora. I stayed in three different homes with families from three different tribes, and the false narrative I had learned in America was replaced with the truth.

My homeland is rich in culture. I loved my culture and the very important ways in which it differed from America.

The Outdooring Ceremony helped me realize how much African Americans were missing out by not having access to one of our most powerful traditions. Not understanding who we are keeps us ignorant of our rich history and disconnected from our traditions. I believe it is this disconnect that fuels our unidentified internal anger and resentment. In our souls, we can feel something is missing. Simply teaching our history as an act of academia is impractical and impersonal. African-Americans need traditions in the form of authentic rituals that will enrich, heal, and mend our fragmentation. Witnessing the richness of ritual and ceremony was healing to my soul and enlightening to my mind.

My education also introduced me to the sacredness of all living things. Brother Ishmael worked with plant medicine (herbalism) and used the power of plants for healing purposes. On several occasions, I accompanied the herbalist to identify and gather certain plants. Before we removed a plant from the ground, we prayed over it, thanking it for giving its life for us. After we extracted the plant from the ground, we offered tobacco as a gift to the earth. Everything is sacred and is to be appreciated and honored and not used indiscriminately. I learned our mission as Divine beings is to take care of the earth and all its inhabitants.

Emergence

Toward the end of my learning journey, Brother Ishmael surrendered his pulpit to me. I was to deliver two sermons for my final assignment. When I stepped onto the pulpit, Spirit descended upon me. I'd never experienced such a mesmerizing feeling which completely humbled me. At that moment, I understood what being filled with the "Holy Spirit" really meant.

In those twenty minutes, I delivered a message others needed in order to uplift their lives. I was being used as a vessel for healing and I GOT IT! A Spiritual Healer is being of service to others. I surrender and let the power and presence of Spirit work through me.

My experiences in Africa revealed the truth of who I am and where I come from. It helped me heal my soul and feel whole. I no longer felt like a ship at sea without a rudder. I was prepared to return carrying a message of hope, and healing.

Did you grow up with rituals? (family dinners, celebrations, etc.)

How did these events influence you?

Do you have rituals that you practice?

Are you familiar with any African rituals?

Do you believe understanding our African rituals could benefit African Americans?

"When a woman is hungry, she says, 'Roast something for the children that they may eat.'"

African Proverb

Part IV

My True Narrative

The Queen Reigns

The woman who returned to America was not the woman who left. I witnessed the power, presence, and richness of the African culture—my culture—and it anchored me in the world. I understood the pain my ancestors suffered, and that it is carried in my DNA. I healed the wounds created by the traumatic experiences birthed from systemic racism. I had indeed (experienced Sankofa) gone back and reclaimed my throne. I could move forward in power.

My awakenings in the homeland gave me a total understanding of what is really going on in America. I saw the truth. The negative characteristics and behaviors we express are created by the racist system we are forced to live within. Black people from the African Diaspora are descended from courageous, loving, and spiritual people. We are not an angry, dysfunctional people.

The systemic racism in the United States propagates lies about who we are. Those lies become our reality, which fuel our powerlessness. Unless we travel away from these untruths and return to our source, it is difficult to feel what has happened to us on a cellular level.

What I experienced in Ghana gave me clarity on who I am as a Black woman from the African Diaspora living in America. Sistahs are powerful. We are the glue that binds the family together. If you destroy our essence, the family will deteriorate. My responsibility is to recognize and stop the destructive tactics used to rob us of power.

Living in America was challenging after being in Africa for a year. When I returned home, I felt anxious, out of sync, and unconformable in public settings. I called Brother Ishmael, and he explained that I had just flown into the largest anger energy field on the planet and had not prepared myself. I was shocked to know in America, I lived with a protective (vibrational) shield around me to survive.

I didn't need protection in Ghana because only love, peace, and acceptance were present, not anger, hatred, and violence, so the shield had dissolved. However, I was vulnerable to destructive forces without that protective shield in America. So, at the request of Brother Ishmael, I returned to Ghana and stayed three months while he fortified me. I returned home able to survive as a Black woman in this violent society.

Stepping Out on Faith

When I returned to work, it was evident my career as a child welfare worker was over. The pain of removing children from vulnerable sistahs was unacceptable. Knowing I had to leave created a new challenge.

Although God had shown me the way out, the thought of leaving my good-paying civil servant job struck fear in the core of my being. I was trapped in the same system my sistahs were. It had brainwashed us all. Some of us believed we were helpless victims. Others believe we were powerful helpers. We both accepted the false narrative; the system was a source we couldn't do without.

This 9-to-5 job was my only way to survive. I worked hard to earn a college degree, and I thought my destiny was to stay here and struggle to help the poor and unfortunate. My co-workers reinforced those beliefs and told me it would be insane to leave. But that voice within was relentless, "Have faith and leave this place! There is work for you to do, and you cannot do it here."

I typed my retirement letter and immediately put it in my desk drawer. Terrified to walk it over to personnel, I sat at my desk, paralyzed with fear. Everyone's words keep repeating in my mind. It was risky to leave the security of a good-paying government job (even if that job was killing me). I was only fifty years old and too young to retire. I would not get full retirement benefits, but I would have medical insurance for life and a small pension. I knew retiring didn't mean I would stop being of service; it only meant I would be of service outside of the department. But the conditioning I received had me STUCK.

In my heart, I knew God had a plan for me. So, I closed my eyes at my desk and prayed for the strength to file my retirement papers. Just then, a co-worker walked up. Everyone considered Miss Arvene, a prayer warrior. Realizing she was my answer to prayer, I shared my dilemma.

Straightforwardly, she said, "If God told you to leave this job, you must leave. No one can take your blessings from you, but you can give them away. God has something much bigger for you to do, even if you can't see it." Seeing the conviction in her eyes and calm voice dissolved my fear and gave me courage.

The next day, I turned in my letter of retirement. And just a few hours later, I received a call from a colleague inviting me to join a national speaking tour for college students. The tour would start one week after I stopped working. I would visit eight college campuses for six weeks and speak to over 3,000 students. My fee would be the equivalent of three months' salary!

Once again, the pain of staying in a situation had become stronger than leaving. I didn't know when I stepped out in faith; I had begun writing my new narrative. A narrative where I would reign as Queen.

Have you stepped out on Faith even though you were afraid?

Were you surprised by how things worked out for you?

How would writing a new narrative for your life be beneficial?

Ida M. Bell

May 27, 1929 - March 4, 2005

Thinking of the impressive qualities of my mother is heartwarming. She generously shared her wisdom, compassion, and love. She demonstrated a strong work ethic and the importance of being responsible. Her loving nature was fully felt throughout my life.

She sacrificed so much for her family. Mom lived her Christian faith in many ways. Frequently, I chuckle to myself about my involvement in volunteerism which emanated from observing my mother's "helping hands" in our community and church.

Mom had such a joy for life. She could talk to anyone. Plus, she was such a good listener and an encourager. She was a strong motivator, constantly pushing me and others to set goals, move forward, and commit to a plan. Her pragmatic way of thinking and practice of plain talking was so appreciated. One of her axioms was, "You must value yourself and recognize your worth."

Mom was a classy and elegant lady who shared so much of her wisdom, strength, compassion, and understanding. I am so blessed and grateful knowing she continues to walk with me.

Justine Bell

Chapter 22

Unexpected Miracles

After taking an early retirement, my dream was to travel the world and be of service to people. My elevator speech was, "I want to travel and run my mouth." While attending a week-long business seminar, I met a woman developing a new program for women entrepreneurs, who offered me a position as a facilitator in her new Core Value training program.

A year later, I was living my dream—traveling the world and running my mouth. The work took me to Singapore, Malaysia, Vietnam, and Las Vegas. While in Vietnam, I participated in and witnessed two miraculous phenomena that showed me firsthand the power of spiritual healing.

In Vietnam, we facilitated a Core Value training for a sizeable multi-level marketing business. Once the workshop was over, the host took us on a trip outside of Ho Chi Minh City to visit the Viet Cong's main encampment during the war. The Vietnamese do not look at the Vietnam war as a civil war between the north and south Vietnam. To them, the war was a fight against a superpower, which they won. They are proud to show visitors the main base where they strategically planned the defeat of America's military, and I was grateful for the opportunity to visit for several reasons.

I've always had strong feelings about the Vietnam War and hoped to visit the country one day. I grew up living next to Hunters Point naval shipyard, where I had access to the base because my father was in the navy. I hung out with the young men returning from Vietnam during the war. In fact, I was even engaged to one.

Many of them suffered from post-traumatic stress syndrome (before we knew what that was), drug addiction, and other mental health issues. They told me stories about how difficult it was for them to fight a war they didn't believe in or want any part of. Some were trained as assassins and found it difficult to fit back into society when they returned home. Worse yet, the military had no deprogramming programs to support their reentry into society. One day they were in the jungles, fighting for their lives. The next day, they walked the streets of America. It was up to them to transition back into civilian life. Some were disconnected from their feelings and used drugs to help them forget the horrors they witnessed and participated in.

Even though I didn't know anyone who died in Nam, I was so close to those young African American soldiers that I felt their pain and grief. They shared stories of leaving friends on the battlefield and feeling guilty because their fallen friends would be forever lost in a foreign country. Although the military told families that the coffins contained their loved one's remains, many didn't. Instead, the caskets of returning soldiers were filled with rocks. Those young men never received a proper burial because their remains never returned home and there was no formal acknowledgment of their sacrifices until 1982, when the Vietnam War Memorial was erected in Washington, D.C.

I wanted to visit the Vietcong encampment because I felt there was a way I could help the thousands of young men who lost their lives on foreign soil. I had no idea how I knew this. I just believed those lost souls needed freedom. With God's guidance, I could offer them help as a Spiritual Healer.

I followed my spiritual intuition and moved forward with my release ceremony, only telling one other person what I was attempting to do in my group. Somehow, this Brother understood what I was trying to do and offered to stand with me. Upon arrival at the site, I said a prayer and walked onto the campground. This was a place where the Vietcong and Americans had fought and died and the feeling there was chilling. I immediately felt unrest within—something I could not explain in words.

The Vietnam government had set up this area as an outdoor museum with a gift shop and mannequins dressed in military gear holding guns arranged around a campsite. It looked eerie. There was a building with an indoor theater showing videos of the war and how the Vietnamese soldiers lived underground on different levels. There was a level for sleeping, one for strategic planning, one for cooking, and a trench by which they traveled. These underground tunnels were hundreds of miles long. That is why the Vietcong could disappear into the jungle and reappear behind the American troops miles away. There was an opportunity to walk the underground trenches, however I declined. Americans are much larger than Vietnamese people, and these small tunnels were made for them, not us. It wasn't an easy walk but several of my colleagues made it through.

There was also a shooting range where you could fire an M-16 rifle, the same weapon American soldiers used in Vietnam. No one in the group wanted to participate, but a voice within directed me to fire one of the weapons. I needed to feel the destructive power that killed the souls I wanted to liberate, and shooting this powerful weapon would connect me to them in a genuine way. I walked to the gun range, paid admission to fire one clip, and said a prayer. When I unloaded the clip at the paper target, the velocity of the bullets leaving the gun was indescribable. It was empty in a matter of seconds. The destructive power of this weapon was terrifying. The shells I fired were the length of my index fingers, and the paper target I fired at was destroyed, indicating that the damage these bullets could do to a human body was cataclysmic.

My traveling companions were puzzled as they watched me fire the weapon. They did not understand why I would want to engage with a weapon of mass destruction. Their confusion was understandable, especially since they knew me as a spiritual person. Unfortunately, I wasn't able to explain my actions to them. Instead, I focused on what I was about to do to free my brothers from their earthly imprisonment.

Walking to a secluded area, I spread my arms wide, closed my eyes, and went into prayer. I thanked each soul for their selfless service and asked forgiveness for taking so long to return for them. I promised that each soldier who perished here would never be forgotten and assured them they were loved. Finally, I invited those spirits to leave this place and offered my body as a doorway. In my mind's eye, I envisioned young men walking toward me and passing through me. I had no idea what I was doing, but I was doing it with a heart filled with love.

When I arrived back at the hotel, I felt off-centered and out of my body and realized those souls passing through my body didn't stop when I left the campgrounds. I could not explain what was occurring and didn't know what to do. My time in Africa had taught me that not all experiences could be understood or explained, that many occurrences were spiritual in nature. This was one of those times I didn't know what to do and needed advice.

I knew Brother Ishmael would know precisely what was happening and what to do, so I called him in Ghana from my hotel room. I explained what I did and how I was feeling. First, he praised me and explained I had provided a superb service for thousands of earthbound souls. By offering myself as a doorway, I had allowed them to leave a place they were trapped in.

Then, he instructed me to lay down on the bed, spread my energy out over the entire earth, and ask all the souls to come through at once. Having learned how to extend my energy while studying with him, I followed his instructions and invited every soul who died in the war and was still wandering in Vietnam to come through and be free. I cried tears of joy, knowing that thousands would finally be at rest. Afterward, I soaked in a tub of warm water and felt peaceful, serene, and centered.

The next day while enjoying a massage, my Vietnamese masseuse started telling me about a recent miracle in the town square. In the middle of Ho Chi Min City, there was a fifty-foot cement statue of the Virgin Mary holding Baby Jesus. She told me Mary was crying and people were coming from all over

Vietnam to witness this miracle. In fact, so many individuals traveled in, the government closed the city down. They were concerned about promoting this miracle and needed to limit the number of people looking at the statue.

I wanted to see what they called a miracle, so I waited until the crowds subsided and walked to the square. When I arrived, I was shocked at what I saw. Looking up at this fifty-foot statue, I could see an obvious line etched into the concrete that resembled a tear stain on the virgin Mary's face. It was impossible to get up that high without using a crane and there was no logical explanation for what I saw. How could this of happened? I understood why it was being called a miracle.

While looking up at this beautiful image of Mary and Baby Jesus, I heard my inner voice say, "She cries tears of joy because of the souls that were released from their suffering. Your selfless service provided the opportunity for them to return to God."

This was such a profound statement and sounded so fanatical I did not dare repeat it to anyone except my friend who stood with me that day. I accepted the crying Virgin Mary as a miracle that followed a spiritual healing event—a spiritual healing event that I felt humbled to have participated in. And I started to believe I could be used as a vessel for healing.

A couple of days later, that belief was solidified when I experienced a second miraculous event.

We visited a monastery for female monks that had been closed for twenty years. The government had just recently opened it, allowing the female monks to return. It was an amazingly beautiful place. I walked to the main sanctuary entrance and stepped inside to hear the most beautiful singing. It sounded like a choir of over 100 people singing acapella. I walked around the building, looking for the singers but didn't see a soul. The music wasn't from a PA system. These were live voices. I asked my colleagues if they had heard the singing, and they hadn't. Finally, I found our interpreter, and she asked the female monks if there were singers in the temple. They looked at each other and started smiling and smiling, gesturing at me. They explained there were no physical singers. What I heard was singing coming from celestial beings. Only certain people could hear them. In our group of ten, only three of us heard the singing.

My experiences in Vietnam confirmed what I had learned on my spiritual journeys. My purpose is to be of service, and I will be guided as to when and how that occurs. After Vietnam, I believed it was time to step into the role of a Spiritual Healer. However, I didn't see what God had in store for me. I never do!

Have you ever experienced a miracle or spiritual healing?

What happened and how did you feel about it?

Do you know of sistahs who are healers?

Are any of them in your ancestral lineage?

Vilma Joseph

November 17, 1932 – July 14, 2014

My mom was my main source of inspiration. She taught me to be independent and create the life that I wanted. She believed that education both academic study and life experiences were the tickets to success.

Mom would often say, "Common sense is not common." She prepared me to live in an unfair world where others would judge me by how I looked and not on who I was.

She was always kind to others and passed that quality onto me. I miss my mom every day.

Thank you, Mom, for showing me how to live as a Queen.

Paula Joseph

"I'm an Exquisite Black Queen! I like, love, and celebrate myself. I don't fit society's beauty standards, but I'm beautiful to me. I know my worth and I respect who I am as a woman. I've got beauty on the inside and that makes me empowered and powerful. I'm fearless and comfortable in my own skin. I've got flaws, but I'm still confident! This Queen right here is flawed yet phenomenal, valuable and unique!"

Angela Davis

Chapter 23

Reclaiming My Queendom

Black women are the guardians of morality, speakers of truth, and examples of Divinity. For, generations we've lived with a false narrative that was created to dimmish our power. America is like the man behind the curtain in the Wizard of Oz. He is a fake and a fraud who sells illusions. Unfortunately, the illusion we were sold hid our brilliance and distorted our reality within a false narrative. It is time to release the Legacy of Silence, speak our truth, heal our wounds, and create a new narrative.

As I continued to accept my role as a Spiritual Healer and take action as I was guided, I found that Spirit began to restore parts of my queendom that had been stolen, subdued, or silenced.

Reclaiming My Gift
The Writer Who Would Not Write

Although I grew up in a household with parents who always encouraged me to move forward in the direction of my dreams there was another narrative running in the background of my sub-conscious. One which went counter to what my parents taught me. It was so pervasive I didn't even realize it was there being the saboteur in my life. After years of hearing this internal dialogue, I unconsciously accepted it was my truth.

As a young girl, my mother enrolled me in a book club and every month, I received a book. I was fascinated by the different ideas I read about and mesmerized by the amazing places I visited through the pages.

Inspired by what I was reading, I began writing short stories about my ideas and submitting them in school, and my writing capabilities flourished under the supervision of encouraging teachers.

My mother was a domestic for a wealthy woman named Mrs. Q, and I would often go with her to work. Mrs. Q, took an interest in me. While my mother worked, I did also. Mrs. Q would give me one of her son's National Geographic magazines and tell me to choose an article, read it, write a report, and then make an oral presentation.

This was an exciting activity for me. It gave me the opportunity to read from different material and show off my skills. I would read the article, use her manual typewriter to type up my work, and then proudly delivery my report. Mrs. Q praised and encouraged me to expand upon my work, eventually giving me her son's collection of National Geographic magazines. Through those magazines, I discovered more about the wonders of the world.

In high school, I received high grades in all of my English classes. In fact, in my freshman year, I was allowed to enroll into a senior year English class where I excelled and outperformed all my senior classmates. I made the decision to attend college, major in English, and one day become a published author. I regularly announced my intention to anyone listening—I was going to be a writer. That idea filled me with so much joy and happiness.

Unfortunately, I had an internal conversation which made me question my ability to be a writer. Who are you to think that you are a writer? Do you know any writers that look like you? You can't be a writer. You're a little Black girl from public housing projects. That voice was so loud, it drowned out all the praise I received and negated all evidence to the contrary. One day, I acquiesced to the lie, put down my pen, and just simply stopped writing. I never discussed my internal conversation it was my secret. But deep within, I wept because I was letting a good part of me go.

That part of me stayed dormant and subdued for thirty-six years.

After retiring from Social Services, I started facilitating transformational workshops for young people, helping them identify the stories that were holding them back from pursuing their dreams. In my work with them, I started to recognize the stories I'd told myself about my ability to write. I remembered that internal narrative that had fueled my decision to stop doing what I loved to do and how I'd abandoned my dream of becoming a published author.

When the opportunity to write a story for the first Chicken Soup for The African American Soul popped up, I seized it without hesitation. It had been over thirty years since I had penned a story but I wrote two stories and submitted them. I ignored that old internal conversation because I recognized it for what it was—a lie. To my delight, out of 2,500 submissions, both of my stories were chosen for publication. With the stoke of a pen, I had written a new narrative for my life. I was a published author.

What is your gift?

Is it being restricted because of the narrative running in the background of your subconscious?

Do you remember telling yourself that your gift, your talent, was not important?

What narrative are you living in that is keeping you from growing and developing and sharing your God-given talent with the world?

Reclaiming My Beauty
Whose Body Am I Living In?

I grew up loving my body. I was slender, physically fit, and just looked good according to the standards of beauty put in front of me. It never occurred to me that my model for beauty was the skinny White women. And although I wasn't White, I was skinny.

I felt physically attractive until I went into a pre-mature menopause after having a complete hysterectomy. My body slowly started to morph into an object I could not recognize as I gained a lot of weight and lost muscle tone. I started a regimen of hormones which helped how I felt but did not improve how I looked. This wasn't a body I recognized or liked, and I started criticizing it and saying ugly things to myself daily.

While looking at myself in the mirror, I called myself names— fat, ugly, unattractive, unfit, etc.—and felt more and more unworthy. I started looking for quick fixes to change my appearance and took every potion, pill, drink, food, and tried every diet that was offered. I purchased larger size clothing, trying to make myself look attractive. On the outside, I looked good and smelled good, but my negative internal dialogue was tearing me down.

The longer I held negative opinions about my body, the less power I had to do anything about it. I no longer had control over my thoughts about my body. The negative narrative filled my sub-conscious and conscious mind. When I looked into the world, I saw that negative narrative reflected back. African American women do not fit society's definition of what attractiveness should look like. I no longer had the body shape of a skinny White woman, therefore I was unattractive. All I needed to do was get the body of my youth back and I would once again be worthy of praise.

The more I tore myself down, the lower I sank into a body depression (extreme sadness about how I look). The depression sent me on feel-good journeys and I did things which made me feel good but were not good for me. I ate fattening foods that put more weight on. I shared my bed with men who didn't respect or acknowledge my worth. I interacted with groups where everyone was competing for the same thing—the opportunity to feel good.

The older I got, the more I realized my health was going to be negatively impacted by my weight. I had a choice to make: continue to engage in behaviors that weakened my body or develop a lifestyle that supported longevity. I wanted to live and be healthy and strong, not weak and sickly.

I remembered that I am a powerful woman and can accomplish anything I set my mind to! My goal to promote optimal health became my focus. There was no quick fix to healthy living and I threw out that old false narrative with all of its standards of beauty and created a new one: A healthy body functioning optimally is a beautiful body.

It was important not to push against the old false narrative but to embrace the new one. Mother Teresa gave us the right way to look at life when she was asked to attend an anti-war rally and said, "No. But I would attend a pro-peace rally." She realized that when you push against something, you strengthen it and weaken yourself. But when you embrace it, you gain strength.

I needed to create positive thoughts about my body and took charge by enrolling in an eighteen-day health retreat—a program that focused on mind, body and soul regeneration.

It provided me with the space to look at my current behaviors and to learn techniques and strategies that would support new ones. When I returned home from that retreat, the work really started.

I changed my diet and I examined my relationship with food. Was I eating because I was sad, lonely, upset, or just wanted to comfort myself? Did this food make me feel good because it makes my taste buds happy? Was I searching for love in that bag of popcorn?

When I really looked deeply into how my body responds, it became apparent that certain foods do not support my body. I needed to exclude certain foods from my diet. In the past, my body had thrived on a vegetarian life style, but I had wandered away from it because a pound cake was way more comforting than a bowl of grapes.

Giving up animal products wasn't easy because I like chicken, turkey, cheese, and bacon; but if I wanted to look and feel better, they had to go. I also went back to making fresh juice daily and exercising on a regular basis. I started to work out with a personal trainer because I needed the discipline to keep at it. Over a year, my body slowly started to respond. I lost inches first, then the bloating in my mid-section went away, and finally my waist returned.

I discovered that when I took on my physical body, I was taking on my entire life. It wasn't just about my diet or my exercise— it was also about my relationship with my sistahs. My ability to meet once a month with women I trust and talk about what was going on in my life empowered me to control my impulse to eat away my uncomfortable feelings.

Because I can verbalize what is going on with me to my sistahs, I am better able to see when I am getting off-track. I stopped refusing to exercise this amazing body because I was no longer tired or unmotivated. My interactions with them eliminated feeling of loneliness and energized me. It is amazing how lonely we can be, even when surrounded by people all the time. And because we don't talk about how we feel, we turn to other behaviors which are detrimental to our well-being.

As I lost weight and gained muscle tone, the negative internal dialogue turned positive. I started to say uplifting comments to myself and my love for me increased, which also helped to increase my desire to stay on target. I went shopping in my closet and found cute clothes I had purchased but never looked good in—you know, those outfits that still have the tags on them. I purposely cleaned out my closet and released all the clothing in sizes I did not want.

Today I have a body that is functioning at optimal levels. It has reached a comfortable weight because I give it what is needed to thrive. I don't hold up someone's else idea of beauty as my target, and my internal dialogue is free of unhealthy patterns of thoughts about me. I am motivated to continue my healthy lifestyle because I can see and feel the results.

What is your relationship with your body?
Where did your idea of beauty originate?

Is food a tool used in your world to (fill in
the blank) _____?

Has the false narrative influenced how you view your body?

Do you have an ongoing internal dialogue about your weight?

Reclaiming My Capacity to Love and Be Loved

I grew up in a household with both parents present, but their relationship was dysfunctional. The patterns of behaviors I learned from their relationship became incorporated into my life. Little girls (and boys) mimic what they see and live life accordingly. I watched my mother accept my father's infidelity by staying quiet, not confronting, and ignoring what she knew was happening. I also watched my mother leave a relationship when physical abuse entered into her life and threatened the health of her child.

Looking at my life, I see a reflection of her life. The same pattern that she inherited from her mother, I've inherited from her.

In my relationships, I would turn a blind eye and not allow myself to see what was right in front of my face. If infidelity was present, I did not see it, nor did I allow myself to hear untruths that were being told to me by my partners. I allowed myself to remain in relationships where there was no integrity, no honor, no respect, and certainly no love.

"A woman is loved according to the character of her man."An African Proverb

For thirteen years, I stayed with a man who didn't have the character to love me the way I wanted to be loved. I knew this but stayed because I was afraid to be alone. He was legally married. Not living with his wife, but still married. And while this went against everything I believed in, I continued anyway, believing this was all that was available to me.

The false narrative (perpetuated by a racist society) about Black men was implanted into my sub-conscious. A good Black man is hard to find. Most of them are in jail, drug addicted, or would be intimidated by my accomplishments. Many were living on the downlow so I couldn't trust them. They were low-income earners, which meant I would probably make more money, causing them to be insecure. Black men would cheat on me because there were so many women available to them and they had an immoral character. If I was lucky enough to meet a Black man that worked, was healthy, didn't physically abuse me, and was sexually active, I better hold onto him. It didn't matter that he did not meet the standards I had for a perfect partner.

With this false narrative influencing my thinking. I gave into fantasy thinking about my situation.

This married man would one day miraculously turn into what I desired. That was absurd because he could only act according to his character. His character, said it was okay to lie, to be disrespectful, and to have no consideration for my feelings. It became clear this man did not have the character to love me as a Queen.

When I started to examine my life, I realized this was an area where I was not living up to my expectations. I was highly educated, accomplished, ministering to others, and yet accepting treatment from a man that did not honor me. It was clear I needed to change my thinking about Black men and relationships. I realized what I was allowing to exist in my life was of my own choosing. I had brought him into my life and I could take him out of it.

First, I needed to let him go. It is also true that no two objects can occupy the same space at the same time. Before I could have my perfect partner, I needed to create space for him. Releasing the man occupying that space was the first step to take. I had walked away from the relationship in the past only to return. It wasn't enough not to stop seeing him physically. I had to release that fantasy about us. My work was all internal. It had nothing to do with him. When I chose me over him and reality over fantasy, I was able to walk away.

The second step was to recognize the conversation playing in my head about Black men was a lie. I had to believe the perfect man was out there looking for me. I needed to prepare myself for his arrival. I also realized before I could be in relationship with the man whose character reflected what I needed, I had to reflect the same character. If I wanted to be loved, respected, honored, and treated with dignity, I had to love, respect, honor and treat myself with dignity. I had to become what I wanted to have. That meant I had to release everything in my life that did not reflect my new narrative.

The fear of being alone had caused me to settle for less than I deserved. Although this situation created anxiety, I was willing to accept that over feeling lonely. I examined why I gravitated toward emotionally and physically unavailable men. This type of relationship allowed me to remain distant and be comfortable because I didn't trust men. To hide the truth from myself, I made up the story I wanted closeness. I poured energy into trying to create something I didn't really want.

When I realized my dysfunctional relationships came from my mistrust of men and fear of intimacy, I started to examine the patterns of generational behavior I had inherited. Each new discovery opened new doors for me. I started to honor my ancestors for their courage and have more respect for who I was. I stopped living in a made-up world and stepped out into the real world, expecting to attract a man with the character I desired. I did not have to go looking for this man. I only needed to shift my beliefs, release my fear, put my faith in God, and step onto my throne as the Queen.

The Arrival of My Perfect Partner

In 2016, I made the decision to visit the White House while my beloved President Barack Obama was still in office. I asked a good friend of mine from the East Coast whether she knew of a place I could stay in Washington D.C. She contacted a friend who most generously offered his home to me.

He picked me up from the airport and asked if I was hungry and wanted to eat. I was and did, so we drove to the restaurant. As we were looking for a parking space, I offered to pay for parking in a lot since he was paying for dinner. He looked at me and said, "I didn't say I was paying for dinner." I started to laugh because that was true. He did not say he was going to pay for dinner. He only asked if I wanted to go eat.

For the next four days, I had an amazing time in Washington D.C. This man took me on several rides on this motorcycle, which I loved. He went with me to the White House and we toured the grounds. All the while, I observed his character and the fact he carried himself with respect, acted with integrity, and lived life fully.

On several occasions I found myself thinking, I like this man. I laughed a lot and was filled with joy the whole time I was there. Although I could feel an attraction between us, he never said anything to indicate he was interested.

On the last day of my stay, when he did actually take me out to dinner, I discovered why he never approached me. He explained that a week prior to my arrival, he had entered a relationship and he only engages with one woman at a time. My first reaction was, Dang, you mean I'm a week too late! My second reaction was, Wow, this is a man with integrity. He respected me and honored his woman.

God had provided me with an example of a man who did indeed have the type of character I desired. Meeting him was a confirmation that Black men with strong characters did exist. I simply had to know that. I left feeling empowered.

It was time to create a space in my mind, my heart, and my house for my perfect partner. My cousin suggested I put things in place for him even before he showed up physically in my space. This will sound crazy, but it worked. I purchased a pair of men's slippers and put them under my bed. I cleared out a dresser drawer so there would be a place for him to put his clothes. And then I purchased a new journal and started to write letters to him in which I would tell him I was waiting for him to enter my life, and I was so happy he was making his way to me.

Writing letters to my future man became a regular practice. It strengthened my belief that one day, the perfect partner would walk into my life. Each letter I wrote filled me with confidence and excitement. I put no time frame on when he would show up, or where he would come from. I simply wrote him letters expressing what a joyous occasion it would be when he arrived.

It became clear when I was unencumbered, living life fully with integrity, I would receive the blessing of being loved by a man who had the type of character I desired.

One day while visiting my family in Bermuda, a facetime call came through and it was my friend from D.C.. I could see by the look on his face he was as surprised as I was, which told me immediately this was not a call he intentionally made. I started laughing and he started laughing and we just said hello and hung up.

He immediately sent a text, saying, "I wonder what the universe is trying to tell us?"

I responded, "The universe is saying, 'Don't you know this woman likes you?'" And then I added, "Do you still have a girlfriend?" When he responded no, I went for it and asked, "Can I be the one?"

He responded with, "Can I be the one?"

I texted back, Absolutely!

We started talking and exploring the possibility of creating a relationship. He asked to come out and visit me, and I was all for that until he said he was going to stay for ten days! I went into a panic. A couple of days is okay to have a visitor but ten days? I took it to God in prayer. The answer I received was, "Ten days is a long enough time for you to know if this is someone you want to be in a relationship with." I agreed to a visit but explained I was not ready for physical intimacy, so he would have to sleep on the couch. Of course, he had no problem with that.

As I was preparing for his arrival, I found that pair of dusty men's slippers I had put under my bed five years earlier. I washed them and prepared to give them to him when he arrived. If they fit, he could possibly be the one. I also came across a list of thirty-two characteristics my perfect partner should have. When I was going through a very horrendous breakup, a good friend had offered me this list and said that when I saw them in a man, I would know he was my perfect partner.

Prior to my visitor arriving, I looked at the date I had started my perfect partner journal. I started the journal Dec. 23, 2015, and he was arriving on Dec. 23, 2019. Exactly four years to the day. My slippers fit him perfectly. He also had all thirty-two characteristics on my perfect partner list. On New Year's Eve of 2020, we became a couple.

When I removed everything in my life that did not serve me, the space for a perfect partner opened up.

We are Queens who deserve to be loved as Queens. The colonizers removed us from our queendom and placed us in captivity, but they did not take our essence. It is time for us to rewrite our narratives and reclaim our queendoms.

Do you find your relationships are not with the type of people you want in your life?

Do you have a picture of your perfect partner?

Do you exhibit the characteristics you want to see in a partner?

Is there space in your life for a partner to show up?

Have you given up on finding your perfect partner?

Erma J. Owens
July 27, 1933 – February,12 2001

Dr. Erma Jean Owens, affectionally known as "Honee," was my confidant, my inspiration, and a motivating force in my life. She proved to me if you believe in you, others will also.

My mom graduated at sixteen and pursued a career in nursing. Moving from Fort Worth, Texas, she worked at Cedar Sinai Hospital in LA. until she courageously took her two children and left an abusive relationship, relocating to Oakland, CA.

I remember her for always being positive. Her willingness to help everyone resulted in us having a Homeless Shelter, Nursery School, and Church. Spreading love freely, everyone felt like her best friend. She believed in family and made time to instill confidence and self-worth in her children.

Mom demonstrated that one can be brilliant, spiritually-driven as a God-loving pastor, while caring for family and earning a PhD. She would often say, "Be the change you want to see," and "You are the thinker that thinks the thoughts that makes your dreams come true!"

Mom, I loved you with all of my heart.

Your Loving Son, Curtis

"Stand up straight and realize who you are, that you tower over your circumstances. You are a child of God. Stand up straight."

Maya Angelou

Chapter 24

A Queen's Ministry

When I use the term ministry, it is not restricted to the areas of religion. I believe that anyone who is of service is engaged in ministry. I didn't understand the full ramifications of ministry before living in Ghana where I witnessed individuals who devoted their lives to helping others in contexts outside of religion. Therefore, ministry in action is a term I coined to describe anyone (using their talents) who is actively involved in helping others.

Looking back, I was always actively engaged in ministry. Something within has always called me to be of service to the world. From the first time I ventured out of my home's shelter as a little five-year-old girl, I wanted to be of service. When I walked into kindergarten and saw how my teacher helped me, I decided that is what I wanted to be—someone who helped little children—and set my goal of becoming a kindergarten teacher.

Although I didn't step into that profession, I devoted my life to serving children. My journey took me to Family Day Care, providing service to children 0 – 2 years old. Then I was a preschool head teacher, supervising fifty-three children (3-5 years old) and seven teachers from three different cultures. After earning a Master of Social Work degree, I worked with distressed families at Child Welfare Services. And finally, I spent years helping teens choose more empowered narratives for their lives.

I never used the term ministry to describe my work, but that is what it was. It has always been about integrating my Humanity with my Divinity. It was easy for me to be of service in those various career settings, but serving as a Spiritual Healer required an entirely different consciousness. I needed to relate on a much deeper level.

My first reaction to being called into "The Ministry" was disbelief and shock. "God, you've got to be kidding." I could not see myself being the minister of a church. But that was not God's intention. Instead, I received special instructions which I did not comprehend.

I wasn't to be ordained in the Church of Religious Science I had attended for over thirty years or any other Christian church. Instead, I would be a minister to everyone regardless of their beliefs. I had no idea what type of minister this was, or how to go about becoming one. But I trusted and God lovingly guided me in the direction I needed to go.

I started telling people what God had called me to do, hoping someone would help me because I know God always sends what we need to fulfill our purpose. One Sunday, I shared my dilemma with the assistant minister, and he said, "Oh, you're talking about an Interfaith Minister. That is what I am." I had never heard the term Interfaith Minister before. He told me about a seminary called One Spirit in Manhattan, New York, that ordained Interfaith Ministers.

Interfaith Ministers are individuals educated in many philosophies and religions who minister to individuals of all beliefs. I realized this was what God was directing me to be. Interfaith Ministers worked with the power and presence of God on all levels and in many forms. That made perfect sense to me. In recovery, I discovered that having a spiritual connection didn't have to be in a religious context. Spirituality is a conscious recognition of our Divinity, not an association with a religion.

I contacted the seminary and learned the current semester had already started but I could join the class late if my application with supporting documents were sent in immediately. I pulled everything together and enrolled. Completing the program was challenging because the school was in New York. I was a distant learner and expected to attend class online once a month (pre-Zoom) as well as travel to New York once a year to attend a week-long spiritual retreat.

The work was exhilarating, challenging, and spiritually enlightening—truly a continuation of my education in Ghana. The curriculum showed me that those who worshiped differently from me were not different from me. Just as my Brother in Ghana had said, we are all One Spirit and live in One Universe with One God.

My classmates represented the religions we studied. There were Catholics, Christians from several denominations, Wiccan, Jewish, Muslim, Metaphysicians, Yogis, Buddhists, Sikhs, Naturalists, Christian Scientists, Quakers, Progressive Christians, agnostics, and atheists. We all studied together for two years, learning about each other and how our beliefs intersect.

My two years of study at One Spirit gave me a new level of acceptance of human beings as Divine Beings. It didn't matter what an individual believed; what mattered was that our Divinity connected us. There is no separation in the Universe.

When brought to this country, African Americans were forced to accept a religion that labeled us inferior. Christianity was used as a means of control, as the most effective way to gain and keep control over people is to control their spirituality. As enslaved people, we were taught our heritage made us a cursed people. We were uncivilized and needed to be converted to Christianity to be saved. Bible passages were used to reinforce the captor's truth that our destiny was to live a life of servitude.

They were wrong. Africans are incredibly spiritual and have ancient beliefs and practices. The descendants of Africans living in the African Diaspora are spiritually connected people. Our deep spiritual connection to the Universe runs in the bloodline. In fact, I believe we endured 400+ years of systemic racism because of our spiritual connection to the Creator.

Our African heritage influences everything we do. Just look at our food, music, self-expression, and worship styles. It is the miseducation about our true heritage that prevents us from appreciating the richness of our African roots and the influence it has on us.

Have you felt an urge to engage in a certain work?

Do you realize that this is your calling into ministry?

Are you willing to answer the call and be of service to the world?

*"What I know for sure is that speaking your truth
is the most powerful tool we all have."*

Oprah Winfrey

Conclusion

Reclaim Your Throne
Break The Silence

Every day, we see history being made as Queens return to their thrones. Black females from the African Diaspora are taking their reign back. A Queen stood proudly as the First Lady of America. A Queen is Vice President. The newest juror on the Supreme Court is a Queen. The third highest position in California, Secretary of State, is held by a Queen. The mayors of San Francisco, Los Angeles, and Chicago are Queens. The Attorney General of Massachusetts is a Queen. Queens are in the forefront of defending freedom in the United States Congress.

Using the blueprints of exceptionalism we inherited from courageous ancestors, we are paving the way to freedom for all. We are no longer uncrowned Queens. We are the Original Queens fulfilling their purpose! The reign of the Original Queen is upon us.

When we join together in community, we share our gifts, enjoy sisterly love, and reclaim our Queendoms. We do not want to forget where we came from, however we do want to release the pain we carry hidden within our secrets. Walking through my pain helped me understand the false narratives that were holding me back. Breaking the Legacy of Silence exposed my secrets and revealed my truth. As a result, I wrote a new narrative and legacy. A legacy that gave younger generations the power to speak up about sexual violations, end physically violent relationships and live a life free of secrets.

The only limitations we have are the ones we accept. Acknowledging our pain collectively increases our strength and awareness. They might have taken our crowns and attempted to keep us powerless, but they could not take away our birthright. We are the Original Queens.

Life began through us and is sustained through us. Standing in our power, we protect, defend and impact the world in ways we don't always recognize. We've received countless blessings through our experiences and those of our ancestors. Today is our time to RISE UP and use them to liberate ourselves and the world.

No More Silence

Grandma had *a bad thing happen* to her and was told to

stay silent.

Grandma's daughter *saw a bad thing happening* and was told

to look away and

stay silent.

Grandma's granddaughter *heard a bad thing happening* and

was told to cover her ears and

stay silent.

Grandma's great-granddaughter, *saw, heard, and had a bad*

thing happen to her and was told, That's the way it is for

Black Women. Accept it and

stay silent.

Grandma's great-great-granddaughter was told,

When you feel, hear or see a bad thing happening, don't

STAY SILENT—SPEAK UP!

*How do you feel about the sistahs who are
stepping into powerful leadership roles?*

Are you ready to step onto the throne and reign as a Queen?

*Are you willing to share your hope, strength,
knowledge, and experience with other sistahs?*

*Do you want to join with other Original Queens
in writing a new narrative for sistahs?*

Defining Moments and Guiding Principles
Life Lessons Learned

Book Discussion Topics

When we examine the decisions we make in life, it becomes clear how the consequences of those decisions have defined our existence. It is from this place of clarity we can begin to make new decisions—decisions which create lives built on our truths and not on our fears or pain.

Chapter 1
Grandma Mary's Story

Defining Moment = What Happened
I learned about Grandma's secrets.

Guiding Principle = What I Decided
I would break the Legacy of Silence
and share family secrets.

Consequences of My Decision

Both my grandmother and my mother lived their lives within the Legacy of Silence, never revealing the pain, humiliation, and suffering they endured at the hands of their husbands to their daughters. That pattern of suffering in silence was passed down, to my older sister and myself. We also lived our lives keeping painful secrets. My female ancestors died taking their secrets to the grave. They never had the opportunity to step outside the Legacy of Silence and be free.

When I broke The Legacy of Secrets and shared information with the younger females in my family, I stopped the practice of passing down generational behaviors that, while they had once kept us safe, now kept us imprisoned to the same painful patterns. I understood why my ancestors held secrets, but that behavior needed to end so that future generations could live a life free of pain-filled secrets.

Chapter 2
Mother Grace's Story

Defining Moment = What Happened
I heard my mother crying in the closet.

Guiding Principle = What I Decided
I would silently endure my pain.

Consequences of My Decision

I received a very powerful message from my mother about how Black women deal with pain. We do not complain but deal with whatever life hands us. I held my pain inside and endured everything in silence. I didn't have the luxury of breaking down or expecting others to take care of me. As a Black female, I had to keep going no matter what.

These beliefs kept me trapped within a dysfunctional marriage for ten years. I did not seek help from others. Asking for help would only weaken me. My strength was defined by how much I could bear pain and still perform. As a result, I looked for relief in drugs and alcohol. That led to a twenty-two-year addiction.

Chapter 3
Sister Almyra's Story

Defining Moment = What Happened
At my sister's grave I apologized for abandoning her when she most needed me.

Guiding Principle = What I Decided
I will not allow my feelings of powerlessness to prevent me from supporting another.

Consequences of My Decision

I give my support regardless of how I may feel. God gives me everything I need to be of service to another.

I learned a hard lesson about myself after my sister passed. I was more concerned about my feelings than how I could support her when she needed me. We all have the right to make decisions about how we want to live. I don't have to agree with your choices, but I can certainly stand with you in your choices. Sometimes I will feel powerless as I offer my strength to another who is in need. And that is okay.

Chapter 3
Sister Almyra's Story

Defining Moment = What Happened
Standing in my sister's house, I looked at her portrait and cried because building her dream house killed her.

Guiding Principle = What I Decided
I would not ignore my health or look to material things, hoping they would make me feel whole.

Consequences of My Decision

I maintain a close watch over my spiritual, emotional/mental, and physical health. I no longer hold pain-filled secrets within by focusing on external distractions. Holding pain-filled secrets can push us to seek comfort in external things. Those external things can be people, places, or things. Unfortunately, none of them will bring us long term relief. They eventually become another source of pain we keep hidden within a secret. Sometimes we are so determined to find relief, we ignore important aspects of our life like our health.

One sure way to live a joyous, happy, and free life is to become willing to break the Legacy of Silence and release ourselves from the pain trapped within our secrets.

Chapter 4
The Battle Cry of a Baby Queen

Defining Moment = What Took Place
My father attacked my mother.
I went into a blind rage and tried to hurt him.

Guiding Principle = What I Decided
I needed to stay in control of my anger because
I could lose control and hurt someone.

Consequences of My Decision

I worked to avoid confrontation at any cost. Rather than run the risk of losing control, I allowed situations to happen which caused me pain. Pain was more acceptable than loss of control.

This decision to stay in control of my anger created challenging situations in my relationships, particularly with men. I would stay silent and not speak up about unacceptable behaviors. Men would say derogatory things and tell blatant lies because they knew I wouldn't confront them. They thought I was afraid of them, but I was afraid of me and what I might do if I got angry.

I believed staying silent would help me stay in control. Unfortunately, this strategy did not work. I eventually would explode, which sometimes ended in physical violence (by me). I also suffered emotionally by not confronting situations immediately.

Over the years, I learned to develop a false persona that scared people away. I looked and acted as if I would become confrontational. They didn't realize I was only bluffing. Unfortunately, my presentation prevented me from developing true intimate connections. No one wants to connect with someone they fear.

As an adult, when I closely examined the reasoning behind that childhood decision, I learned that the loss of control I was trying so desperately to avoid was the fight or flight reaction. When I saw my mother under attack, the fear of seeing her hurt threw me into protect mode and I got ready to fight. I didn't understand that not reacting to my feeling was an option.

With that clarity, I released the need to stay in control. I understood it is perfectly okay to get angry, be annoyed, and confront wrong behavior without fear of annihilating someone.

Chapter 4
The Battle Cry of a Baby Queen

Defining Moment = What Took Place
I learned my female ancestors were fierce
warriors and resisted the colonizers.

Guiding Principle = What I Decided
I will always courageously fight injustices.

Consequences of My Decision

When I realized my female ancestors in Africa resisted the colonizers, a new level of pride emerged, expanding my sense of self. I started to walk a little taller, hold my head a little higher, and completely ignore America's propaganda that African Africans are defective.

Unfortunately, like so many young Black girls, I grew up not knowing I was the direct descendent of Queens. My education in this country only taught the history of captivity. Every other immigrant living in this country besides African Americans can turn around and say, "I came from that village, in that town, in that country." They can say, "My great-great-grandmother or my great-great-grandfather was this person in my country." They carry a sense of pride and connectedness, but African Americans were kept from holding onto their history.

Even though I always felt the urge within to push against racism and fight for my rights, I did not realize resistance was part of my ancestral heritage—a heritage I could be proud of.

Chapter 5
It Didn't Have to Be This Way

A Defining Moment = What Happened
I saw Black people in Bermuda living freely and exercising personal power.

Guiding Principle = What I Decided
I could do and be anything I wanted.

Consequences of My Decision

I made life decisions that were not influenced by the racist policies in this country. I enrolled in college and continued until I earned my Doctorate. I opened a successful business, retired at fifty years old from my 9 -5 job, and traveled the world.

I did not accept the narrative that African Americans are incapable of creating self-sustaining communities. Systemic racism is responsible for our collective economic standing. We can't pull ourselves up by our bootstraps if someone has their boot on our neck.

My experiences in Bermuda taught me how to live in this country freely. It helped me understand the conditions in America aren't representative of how Black people live everywhere.

Chapter 6
Domestic Terrorism

Defining Moment = What Happened
Four little girls who looked just like me were murdered
in Church by White men just because they were Black.

Guiding Principle = What I Decided
I needed to always be on alert because Black
people in America weren't safe, even in Church.

Consequences of My Decision

I stopped trusting White people on that dreadful day. Standing in the face of fear and anger, I joined with others and pushed against systemic racism. Not knowing it, I was pulling on that resistance gene in my DNA. I've been moving forward in the face of no agreement all my life, holding the memories of those little sistahs deep within my heart.

The story about this experience is published in Chicken Soup for The African American Soul. I wanted everyone to remember the day they were murdered and how that made us feel.

Chapter 7
Accidental Homicide

A Defining Moment = What Happened
My fourteen-year-old school mate was shot in the back
by a White policeman.

Guiding Principles = What I Decided
It was my fault Matthew died because I did
not make him return to school with us.

Consequences of My Decision

I was overwhelmed with shame and guilt after Matthew died. In my young mind, I had failed him. If I had just tried harder to change his mind, he would be alive. I had no one to discuss my feelings with and my guilt became a secret that altered my worldview.

I started to believe it was my duty to make sure people made the right decisions in their lives. I became super controlling. When others didn't listen to my good advice, I resorted to manipulation. As a result, my relationships were strained and many times contentious.

Eventually, I learned individuals will make decisions based on what they think is best for them. I don't have the power to control another's life. The only power I have is over my decisions. I can stand by individuals as they face the consequences of their decisions, or I can walk away.

Chapter 8
From the Frying Pan into the Fire

Defining Moment = What Happened
My step-dad didn't deny he only pretended
to like me so my mom would marry him.

Guiding Principle = What I Decided
I would stop trusting adults because they lie
and will use you for their own purpose.

Consequences of My Decision

As a young girl, I stopped trusting adults and that carried over into my young adulthood and adulthood. I didn't believe what others said was true or accept their behaviors as real. I was suspicious of everyone's motives toward me.

My biggest fear was having someone use me for their own personal gain again. I hid my true feelings, fearing I might get hurt. The mistrust that started with my stepfather permeated all aspects of life. It influenced my relationships, preventing me from developing deep connections with others.

Chapter 8
From the Frying Pan into the Fire

Defining Moment = What Happened
I watched my house go up in flames.

Guiding Principle = What I Decided
My life was more important than
my material possessions.

Consequences of My Decision

The experience of almost losing my life shifted my priorities. After the fire, I started to put more importance on what I did rather than what I had. I treated my friends differently and stopped feeling superior to them because I had more things than they did.

Having my house destroyed by a fire was a blessing because it changed me. It broke my attachment to material things. My self-worth stopped being tied to my possessions. I believe it also prevented me from growing into a materialistic, selfish, self-centered adult.

Chapter 8
From the Frying Pan into the Fire

Defining Moment = What Happened
My stepfather deliberately took from
me, and I felt powerless.

Guiding Principle = What I Decided
I needed to protect myself and
never feel powerless again.

Consequences of My Decision

That decision to never feel powerless became an obsession
with me. In all circumstances, I worked to maintain power. The
fear of having someone take from me was my motivating force
to always have control over my environment. I never placed
my security in someone else's hand.

When I married, I would not allow my husband to pay the
mortgage. My fear was that one day, he could decide to take
the house, leaving me homeless. This was totally irrational
thinking because my name was on the mortgage.

This same fear of powerlessness carried over into other
relationships (after my divorce). I continued to take on more
responsibilities than I needed to, creating conflict with my
partners. I would refuse to allow them to contribute, believing
that if I did, they would come back and take something from me.

To me, I was just being independent. But I was really being
insecure. This insecurity became the underlying theme
in my life.

Chapter 9
Innocence Stolen

Defining Moment = What Happened
My stepfather said he would teach me about sex.

Guiding Principle = What I Decided
I could not trust a man, no matter who he was.

Consequences of My Decision

Living within the Legacy of Silence prevented my mom and I from talking about what occurred. This was a secret that was never to be addressed. The realization that my body could be used by a man for his desire shattered my innocence and made the world feel more unsafe. I became super protective over my body. And determined I would make the decision about who touched my body and when.

During my teens, I hung out with a lot of people, did a lot of drugs, and avoided having sex. No man would ever get the chance to use me. When I did become sexually active, it was a conscious decision I made. I was the one using his body. He wasn't using mine.

Chapter 10
The Death of a Community

Defining Moment = What Happened
el-Hajj Malik el-Shabazz (Malcolm X) and Martin Luther King Jr. were assassinated for standing up and speaking out against systemic racism.

Guiding Principle = What I Decided
I would fight for the rights of Black people and do it undercover. I would not become a statistic!

Consequences of My Decision

My decision not to become a statistic caused me to be cautious about where I went, who was around me, and what I said. With both el-Hajj Malik el-Shabazz and Martin Luther King being assassinated, the realization hit me that anyone who spoke up and stood up against America's racist system could become a statistic.

My world could be taken away from me any time because there were many people who were listening to what was being said in the community and it was being reported back to those who could hurt us. No one was immune.

I joined forces with others when I could and worked on community projects, always staying under the radar. I did not engage in conversations with individuals I did not know. The 60s were a very turbulent time, in which many of us lived in an emotional state some would call paranoia. However, I called it being smart and cautious. That was how I survived the 60s. Many of my friends weren't so fortunate.

Chapter 11
I Know Who I Am

Defining Moment = What Happened
A White man looked me in the face and said I was only good enough to serve the world as a secretary.

Guiding Principle = What I Decided
I would never allow a White person to define me or prevent me from achieving my goals.

Consequences of My Decision

I stayed prepared to move past the roadblocks constructed by systemic racism. I spent hours creating strategic plans for reaching my future goals. It was important that I stayed on track always. I learned early that if I was going to be successful, I had to be an overachiever just to stay competitive.

I never succumbed to the flattery by good-intentioned White people—that I was an asset to my race. What they really meant was, I didn't pose a threat and would be allowed to stay around. But if I ever stepped off that path and threatened the status quo, the opportunity to stay would vanish.

Chapter 12
A Self-Fulling Prophecy

Defining Moment = What Happened
My best friend Laura was brutally murdered.

Guiding Principle = What I Decided
I never wanted to feel this type of pain again, so
I would never love anyone completely again.

Consequences of My Decision

That one decision to never love completely put an impenetrable wall around my heart. A wall which prevented me from creating intimate relationships. A barrier which constructed emotional distance between me and others. I constructed a life where it was acceptable to love partially. A life where being alone was acceptable.

Chapter 13
A Death

A Defining Moment = What Happened
I filed for divorce and let my old life die.

Guiding Principle = What I Decided
I would release my secrets and
begin a new pain free life.

Consequences of My Decision

I stopped using my energy to hold my old life together and started using it to build a new life. I began releasing the secrets which held me hostage within The Legacy of Silence. The further I moved away from that old life, the stronger I became. With each new step, my courage increased and the fear dissipated.

As new opportunities opened, my life took on new meaning. The present was no longer colored by my past. My future wasn't a projection of memories but of possibilities. I woke up from my nightmare and started to live, not just exist.

Chapter 14
A Rebirth

Defining Moment = What Happened
I admitted to myself I had a drug problem.

Guiding Principle = What I Decided
I would go into recovery and create a drug-free life.

Consequences of My Decision

I felt a sense of freedom after facing my addiction. Up until that point, I saw no way out. It felt hopeless. I was destined to live a life hiding the fact that every day of my life I had to put a mood-altering substance in my body just to function.

For years, I hid the shame-filled secret of my drinking and drug use. I used these substances to mask the pain from years of living with trauma. But now, there was a ray of hope. As I started to release the secrets, hope entered my world. Finally, I had the chance to reclaim my life and live without using drugs and hiding secrets.

Chapter 15
Life as Possibility

A Defining Moment = What Happened
I shook the hand of my hero, President Nelson Mandela.

Guiding Principle = What I Decided
I could live from possibility instead of from past trauma.

Consequences of My Decision

Shaking the hand of President Nelson Mandela was a highlight and a turning point in my life. From that day forward, I did not allow my negative self-talk or the opinions of others to stop me from reaching my dreams.

It did not matter if it looked impossible. Having faith in God and in myself, I could accomplish whatever I wanted to. Meeting my hero put me on a path to living a life I never dreamed of. I visited countries I had only read about, met people I admired, and went on exciting adventures.

The only limitation on my life today is the limitation I put there. It does not matter where I was born or the circumstances surrounding my childhood. I do not have to allow anything to dictate what my future can look like. Life is to be lived freely and abundantly. Today if I can see it as a possibility, I know God and I can make it happen.

Chapter 16
The Africa Trip

Defining Moment = What Happened
I paid a high price for caring excess baggage
with me on my trip to Africa.

Guiding Principle = What I Decided
I would stop caring unneeded stuff
with me, on trips and in Life.

Consequences of My Decision

I realized much of my suffering came from my inability to release those things I no longer needed. The decision to stop dragging around unwanted and unneeded things has allowed me to live an unburdened life. I held onto things, scared I wouldn't have enough. My fear was rooted in childhood experiences and a lack of faith that God would provide for me.

It is not necessary for me hold on to people (pain-filled relationships), places, or things. My first exercise in releasing stuff resulted in me removing fifteen large bags of perfectly good clothing from my one-bedroom apartment. That clothing was more useful in the closets of women who needed them than under my bed. Letting go of a thirteen-year relationship that wasn't serving me created space for my perfect partner.

When I let go and release what no longer serves me, I make room for new and exciting opportunities to show up. When my life is unburdened, I have more energy to love, laugh, play, and enjoy myself.

Chapter 17
"Ubuntu" My Sistah's Pain is My Pain

Defining Moment = What Happened
My actions created pain for a sistah.

Guiding Principle = What I Decided
I would stop working for a system
that damaged Black families.

Consequences of My Decision

The decision to retire from my position as a child welfare worker was a blessing. Working outside of the system, I am free to support Black families according to the dictates of my heart, not the dictates of a racist system. I no longer struggle to work within a system designed to disenfranchise Black families.

Being a facilitator in transformational workshops for young people and an Interfaith Minister has been life-changing. In these roles, I am truly able to be a catalyst for good. I exercised my right to help as I see fit. In my work with Black women, I am fulfilled.

Chapter 17
"Ubuntu" My Sistah's Pain is My Pain

Defining Moment = What Happened
I retired early from my position as
a child welfare worker.

Guiding Principle = What I Decided
I would not be afraid to pursue my dream.

Consequences of My Decision

When I had the courage to follow my dreams and leave a job
that was harming me, I received a blessing I could never have
imagined. For the second time in my life, leaving a situation
that did not serve me gave me a more fulfilling life.

Chapter 18
The Spiritual Healer

A Defining Moment = What Happened
My co-facilitator of a woman's empowerment group slept with my man.

Guiding Principle = What I Decided
I would never betray another sister.

Consequences of My Decision

As a Black woman, I am in a constant battle against forces that would harm me. It is important I do not become an obstacle on the pathway of a sistah. Understanding that betrayal is a destroyer keeps me truthful first to myself and then to others.

Pain is a contributing factor in developing dysfunctional behaviors. It is my responsibility to live a life free of pain and secrets. This is my assurance of always being honest and truthful. Standing in a place of integrity, I can offer my hand to sistahs who are in need.

Chapter 18
The Spiritual Healer

A Defining Moment = What Happened
A woman said I healed a physical condition in her body.

Guiding Principle= What I Decided
I would surrender and accept my role as a healer.

Consequences of My Decision

Surrendering means walking by faith, not by sight. It means trusting and having the courage to keep moving forward into the unfamiliar. It also means listening closely so that the voice of Spirit can be heard.

Even though I wanted to be in total control of my life, I realized when I surrendered and gave up control, my life would become unrecognizable. I did not know where I would go or what I would do. However, I had faith that I would be guided toward a pathway leading to my purpose.

Chapter 19
The Healing Journey

Defining Moment = What Happened
Three different African Healers gave me the
exact same message: I am a Spiritual Healer.

Guiding Principle= What I Decided
I would not run from my calling but allow
Spirit to guide me further into it.

Consequences of My Decision

Being raised inside of traditional religious beliefs made it extremely difficult not to run away from beliefs I did not understand. I wanted to put on my Nikes and "get ghost," but my decision to not run and the overwhelming heartfelt desire to fulfill my purpose made me stay put.

My commitment to be all that Spirit wanted me to be reinforced my decision. The knowledge that one day I would truly be an inlet and outlet for good sustained me.

Chapter 20
A Home Going

Defining Moment = What Happened
I arrived in Ghana, West Africa.

Guiding Principle = What I Decided
I would embrace my heritage and
learn everything I could.

Consequences of My Decision

Every day I lived in Ghana was a day of discovery. Immersed in the culture, I learned who I was, what I was, and why I was. I returned home as a whole person, connected to her roots. I gained an understanding of my place in the Universe.

Chapter 21
Understanding The African Heart

A Defining Moment = What Happened
I stood in The Door of No Return
and felt my ancestor's pain.

Guiding Principle = What I Decided
I would remember and honor my ancestors.

Consequences of My Decision

Prior to my trip to Elmina castle, I had no knowledge or understanding of the suffering my ancestors experienced before they left home forever. My decision to remember them allowed me to embrace my African heritage on a much deeper level. I stopped feeling fragmented and broken and started living with a profound sense of racial pride. I learned the power of ceremony and ritual to keep them near to my heart.

I am not just the descendant of former slaves. I reject America's false narrative that my history started in this country.

Chapter 21
Understanding the African Heart

A Defining Moment = What Happened
I experienced an Outdooring Ceremony—
the African ritual which acknowledges new life.

Guiding Principle = What I Decided
I would create ritual in my life and share its
importance with my brothers and sistahs.

Consequences of My Decision

Creating a space for ritual and ceremony in my life keeps me connected to my African heritage. It allows me to pay homage and respect to the ancestors. Having a connection to the past strengthens me in the present and creates hope for the future.

With the knowledge I gained about the importance of ritual, I've been able to pass it on. Ritual can provide future generations with a concrete way to stay connected to their heritage. As an elder, it is my responsibility to pass knowledge down so that we as a people can be strengthened.

Chapter 22
Unexpected Miracles

Defining Moment = What Happened
In Vietnam, I witnessed two miracles.
I saw a statue of the Virgin Mary weep.
I heard the voices of celestial beings singing.

Guiding Principle = What I Decided
I do believe in miracles.

Consequences of My Decision

I live in a spiritual world and a physical world. When I embraced both worlds, I started living as a Spiritual Healer.

There are many events that we cannot explain using our intellectual knowledge. The decision to embrace those events that are inexplicable has deepened my faith and increased my capacity to love.

Chapter 23
Reclaiming My Queendom

Defining Moment = What Happened
I had two stories published in Chicken Soup for The African American Soul.

Guiding Principle = What I Decided
Writing is my gift and I will share it with the world.

Consequences of My Decision

When I acknowledged my gift to write, I embraced my purpose. Writing allows me to share messages from Spirit. Using my gift can be a blessing in the life of another. My life experiences can help someone meet and overcome a challenge.

Everyone has a special and unique gift from God. Our task is to identify that gift and then share it with the world. When we acknowledge who we are and what we have, our lives take on a deeper meaning. It is not necessary to go looking for our purpose. It is right here with us. We only need to stop listening to external voices and concentrate on that one small internal voice.

Chapter 23
Reclaiming My Queendom

Defining Moment = What Happened
I looked at the New Year picture and felt ashamed.

Guiding Principle = What I Decided
I would reclaim my body so I could
feel good about me again.

Consequences of My Decision

I set a new goal that on my 70th birthday, I would look and feel amazing. At my 70th birthday celebration, I wore a dress that had been hanging in my closet for five years. I liked it but didn't feel good about how I looked wearing it. The dress had become a "one day (when I lose weight) I will wear it" outfit. I was elated when the ONE DAY finally arrived and I took my dress off the hanger and put it on my beautiful body.

Chapter 23
Reclaiming My Queendom

Defining Moment = What Happened
I met a Black man with the character to
love me how I deserved to be loved.

Guiding Principle = What I Decided
I would stop being afraid and accept love into my life.

Consequences of My Decision

When I evicted fear from my life, love was able to move in. My new tenant (love) provides everything my heart space desires and deserves. Today, I am loved according to the character of my man.

Chapter 24
A Queen's Ministry

Defining Moment = What Happened
I received the call into ministry.

Guiding Principle = What I Decided
I would answer the call.

Consequences of My Decision

Answering the call to ministry has enriched my life. There is no greater pleasure in life than working to serve humanity. Being in service to others has increased my capacity to love and feel God's grace. I have the pleasure of offering individuals support in reaching their life goals.

Through my ministry, I am a conduit for Spirit—an inlet and outlet for good.

You're Invited

The Original Queens Sacred Community

I did not transform my life and move from victim to victory alone. I had six powerful Queens standing with me. For over thirty-five years, we nurtured, loved, supported, and encouraged each other to reclaim our thrones. I want to offer the bond (love) of sisterhood to every woman ready to reclaim her throne and live as the Queen she is.

Breaking the Legacy of Silence is not an event. It is a journey— one which cannot be taken alone. When healing past pain and trauma, one needs to feel unconditional love. Our ancestors understood the power of sistahhood and community. They used their love for each other to create sacred spaces that sustained their survival.

Standing on the shoulders of our ancestors and holding hands, we can guide each other out of the dark world of secrets into the daylight of truth. It is my dream to offer the Original Queens Sacred Community as a safe space-a haven where you can reveal (your truth), heal (your pain), reclaim (your power), and share (your strengths).

I invite you to join The Original Queens Sacred Community and embark on a new journey with us. Together, let's create new narratives, break patterns of generational behaviors, and build foundations that support those young sistahs coming behind us. They deserve to step powerfully into a future filled with promise unburdened by the past. We can make that happen by sharing our truth.

The Original Queens Sacred Community is our gathering place. Together we can reclaim our thrones, speak with active voices, and step back into our Queendoms. Let us rise together!

Ubuntu, my Sistahs!

I am because you are. And you are because I am. We walk together as one.

originalqueens.net

About Dr. Rev. Ahmondra McClendon

Dr. Rev. Ahmondra McClendon is an Interfaith Minister, Progressive Christian Minister, Trainer, Inspirational Speaker, Published Author, Spiritual Mentor/Advisor, and Certified Master Facilitator.

She holds a Master of Social Work Degree from San Francisco State University and a Doctor of Ministry Degree from New York Theological Seminary.

With over thirty-five years of experience in the field of social work and human services delivery, she is sensitive to the human condition. Although her life is in harmony today, it wasn't always. For many years, she was trapped in a world of drug-addiction, domestic violence, molestation, homicide, and poverty.

For a decade, she existed behind a wall of silence in a world filled with pain-filled secrets, all the while acting as if everything was okay. She was a victim of her circumstances, surviving in a world of fear and uncertainty.

Realizing her circumstances did not determine her future, Dr. Rev. Ahmondra McClendon broke The Legacy of Silence, a generational pattern of behavior passed down to Black women, and made herself the most important person in her life.

Today she works to create sacred spaces where Black women can speak their truth and reclaim their power. In her new book, The Uncrowned Queen Reclaims Her Throne When a Black Woman Breaks the Silence, she courageously reveals her stories of abuse and misuse on her ancestral tree. Providing a window into the secret world where generations of Black women have suffered in silence allows others to understand why they live with silenced voices and hurting hearts.

Through historical accounts and personal experiences, Dr. Rev. Ahmondra McClendon offers the truth sistahs have been seeking. She reveals the true narrative of The Original Queens and Mothers of Civilization along with insight into breaking old patterns and developing new ways to thrive, dream, and rejoice. She provides a pathway to personal liberation and freedom.

Dr. Rev. Ahmondra McClendon believes when we speak our truth and navigate the waters of personal challenges, we can create a life we love and love the life we live.

Dr. Rev. Ahmondra is available for spiritual counseling, workshops, seminars, keynotes, and book signings as well as specialized events such as spiritual joinings, weddings, home goings, baby dedications, house blessings, etc.

www.DrAhmondra.com
www.circleofconsciousness.com

Ingram Content Group UK Ltd.
Milton Keynes UK
UKHW020857040423
419625UK00014B/809